THROUGH THE DEVIL'S GATEWAY

THROUGH THE DEVIL'S GATEWAY

Women, Religion and Taboo

Edited by
Alison Joseph

SPCK

in association with
Channel Four Television Company Limited

First published in Great Britain 1990
SPCK
Holy Trinity Church
Marylebone Road
London NW1 4DU

in association with
Channel Four Television Company Ltd
60 Charlotte Street
London W1P 2AX

© Alison Joseph 1990

All rights reserved. No part of this book may be reproduced or transmitted in any form or by any means, electronic or mechanical, including photocopying, recording, or by any information storage and retrieval system, without permission in writing from the publisher.

British Library Cataloguing in Publication Data

Through the devil's gateway: women, religion and taboo.
   1. Women. Attitudes of religions
   I. Joseph, Alison
291.178344

ISBN 0-281-04467-8

Typeset by Cambridge Photosetting Services
Printed in Great Britain by Courier International, Tiptree, Essex

Contents

The Contributors   vi

Introduction   1
Alison Joseph

1 Women's Body and Blood: The Sacred and the Impure   7
Rosemary Radford Ruether

2 'In thy blood live': Gender and Ritual in the Judaeo-Christian tradition   22
Leonie J. Archer

3 Divine Mother or Cosmic Destroyer: The paradox at the heart of the ritual life of Hindu women   50
Sanjukta Gupta Gombrich

4 Rose of Lima: Some thoughts on purity and penance   60
Sara Maitland

5 The Castration of Women: Nineteenth-century women and the legacy of biological determinism   71
Alison Joseph

6 The Jewish Woman: Different and Equal   87
Linda Sireling

7 Apart From or A Part Of: The place of celibacy   97
Lavinia Byrne IBVM

The Contributors

ROSEMARY RADFORD RUETHER is a Roman Catholic feminist theologian, author or editor of over twenty books on social justice and Christian theology, and professor of Applied Theology at Garrett Theological Seminary and Northwestern University in Evanston, Illinois.

LEONIE J. ARCHER was until last year fellow in Jewish studies of the Graeco-Roman period at the Oxford Centre of Postgraduate Hebrew studies, and member of Wolfson College. She has now moved on to work on environmental issues. She has published extensively, most recently *Her Price is Beyond Rubies* (Sheffield Academic Press 1990) on Jewish women's lives in antiquity.

SANJUKTA GUPTA GOMBRICH taught Indian philosophy and religion at the University of Utrecht, Netherlands. After retirement she has moved to Oxford. She has published six books on Indian philosophy and Hindu religions and many monographs and articles on Indian philosophy, religion and the position of Hindu women in their own society.

SARA MAITLAND was born in 1950 and now lives in east London. She has published extensively in areas of feminism and theology. Most recently, her novel *Three Times Table* has been published by Chatto.

ALISON JOSEPH is a film maker and co-director of the independent production company Works on Screen. She has written various articles and several screen plays. She lives in London with her husband and two-year-old son.

LINDA SIRELING is a housewife and freelance writer. She lives in north-west London with her husband and three children. Ten years ago she became much more religious, having been up till then quite unobservant and uneducated in Judaism.

LAVINIA BYRNE is a member of the Institute of the Blessed Virgin Mary. She works at the Institute of Spirituality, Heythrop College, University of London, where she co-edits *The Way*. She is the author of *Women Before God* and *Sharing the Vision*, both published by SPCK.

Introduction

In the major religions of the world, women seem to fare rather badly. The Proverbs of the Old Testament return over and over again to the theme that men should beware women; the Jewish Talmud says that if you teach the Laws to a woman, you teach her lasciviousness; the Hindu sage Manu teaches that if women go unrestrained, the result is anarchy; and the oft-quoted Church Fathers and medieval theologians appear to respond to the idea of the Female with fear and disgust. It was Tertullian who said that women are 'The Gateway of the Devil'.

The main message seems to be that women, for whatever reason, are less able to aspire to higher spiritual states than men. Generally this state is to do with basic physical facts surrounding women's ability to give birth, which equates them with the animal side of Man's state; or with Nature rather than Culture.

But Nature and Culture are by no means absolute in their antithesis, but are themselves culturally mediated. Neither has the polarity between Male and Female which we so take for granted ever been based on rock-solid foundations, but has depended on a variety of shifting meanings.

Into these debates, therefore, the issues surrounding women and religion introduce their own questions and analyses. There is, of course, one simple critique, which says that in a religion which sees God as male, and where only men are allowed in the holiest places, there is clearly no place for women. This has spawned a fragmented movement of new religions which worship a female divinity.

This however ignores the fact that huge numbers of women are born into religious traditions, find their cultural identity within them, raise their families according to them. And even for those women who turn to religion later in their lives, the Goddess, whatever her ancient roots, exercises a weaker pull than the long-established structures that are culturally familiar.

In Christianity, it has become a problem for many believers that the masculinity of the doctrine is stressed and the feminine aspects marginalized. Yet rather than desert their tradition, people have begun to search within the myths and rituals of their religion for interpretations that redress this balance.

Rosemary Radford Ruether has worked in this way within Catholicism and the American 'Woman-church' movement. In this book she shows how in the years of the establishment of the Christian Church, holiness came to be defined by the exclusion of the female, and a concept of purity which had its roots in the Old Testament was used to establish the priesthood as a wholly male structure.

This will be familiar to anyone who has followed the debates over the last few years concerning the ordination of women within the Anglican Church. The language used in Synod has often proved to be less than gentlemanly. In Synod, it was declared that to admit women to the priesthood would be like admitting a virus into the bloodstream. More recently, the language of the environmental movement has been employed to invoke a sense of the impending 'pollution' should women be ordained.

This imagery is even more extraordinary when one considers that in this country, the Christian Churches[1] are among the few places of worship where women can go whether they are menstruating or not. No one, apparently, is interested. The Christian Church is alone in no longer having prescribed ritual to do with childbirth and menstruation. The fragments that remain take the form of the ceremony of the Churching of Women after childbirth, that is, that after forty days of confinement, the woman goes to church for a ritual to mark her return to the community. But everyone is keen to say that it is hardly ever used now.

Are we to conclude, therefore, that the Anglican Church's neglect of purification ritual for women is not because it believes women to be 'clean', but because it would rather such matters weren't mentioned at all?

Every culture has a concept of purity. Whether we avoid certain foods because God has told us to, or whether it's simply because of the E numbers; whether our purification rituals are there to chase out demons in the name of spiritual purity, or germs in the name of hygiene . . . we all have a sense that beyond the boundaries of our lives lurks Chaos. The transgression of boundaries is potentially dangerous. Mary Douglas has dealt with this extensively in *Purity and Danger*[2], where, amongst other sources, she looks at the Book of Leviticus in these terms. In order to enter the Temple, one must be pure; in order to be pure, the boundaries of one's own body must not have been transgressed with anything impure. Women, because of their cycles of menstruation and childbearing, are impure more often than men.

In this book, Leonie Archer looks at the effects of this in the Judaism of antiquity, where blood has a major significance in ritual both in the sacrifices in the Temple and in the shedding of blood in circumcision – the 'Covenant' between God and his people. The blood of the Covenant continues to have a central place within the Christian communion. Yet, as Dr Archer explains, the uncontrolled bleeding of women has a negative value.

Where blood has a significance, and menstrual blood negatively so, women are granted a kind of power. In Hinduism there is a burden placed on women to be responsible for protecting the community from their potential 'pollution'. Sanjukta Gupta Gombrich shows how at the heart of women's place within Hinduism, lies a basic paradox. Within a healthy tradition of Goddess-worship, there is assigned to the Goddess an ambivalence, a sense that left to herself she will be destructive rather than nurturing. This double view of the female has repercussions within the lives of Hindu women.

Perhaps because Christianity has no law as such, the concept of purity became veiled behind ideas of spiritual goals rather than being simply defined by physical states. Sara Maitland looks at its complexity, in particular with regard to the sixteenth-century saint Rose of Lima, who appears to have inflicted injuries on herself in a most appalling way. This essay untangles what we know of Rose of Lima from modern concepts of anorexia, neurosis or masochism, or the easy definitions of patriarchal oppression through which contemporary interpreters are tempted to explain the penances of women saints.

In the next essay too, the concept of the female body as a site for conflict is taken up again, in an examination of nineteenth-century medicine and its view of the female. The emergent medical profession of the nineteenth century created a biological view of the female to which we still cling. And it might even be said that it is from this, far more than from early Christianity, that we have inherited our sense of the dubious physical nature of the female, and our idea that the human norm is male and that to be female is in itself a pathological state.

It is a paradox too, that because Christianity has been able to drop any mention of the physical cycles of women's lives, secular culture has ended up with an idea that true liberation means we can forget 'those difficult days', and 'carry on as normal'; assuming, perhaps, that to be normal is to be more like a man.

Penelope Shuttle and Peter Redgrove, in their book, *The Wise Wound*[3], show how the taboos surrounding menstruation in western culture are just as oppressive (perhaps even more so) as those of religious structures which lay down washing rituals. For Christian silence on the subject, combined with our nineteenth-century medical heritage, has resulted in a culture where menstruation is to be treated as a problem or ignored altogether.

The Shuttle/Redgrove thesis states that periods have meaning, and we ignore it at our peril. And indeed, it is surely the case that menstruation is a profound event, the other side of ovulation, the balance to fertility as well as the mark of it.

This view will hold no surprises for orthodox Jewish women. Every month they mark their cycle with a ritual bath, the *mikva*, having been sexually unavailable to their husbands for as much as two weeks before that. In this book Linda Sireling writes about its significance in Judaism, and in her life. The Old Testament word *tameh*, usually translated as 'unclean', in fact means separate, or set apart. In Judaism, a menstruating woman is not dirty or tainted; she is simply in another state, set apart and unavailable.

Non-availability is an idea deeply embedded in the Christian tradition of celibacy; though for too long now it has been seen as renunciation by men of sinful life, rather than as a radical statement by women. Yet for women religious, celibacy has come to be a statement in direct opposition to western cultural norms of women having to be available to men and usually defined by their relationships to them. Lavinia Byrne here examines the tension within the life of a nun, both set apart yet belonging to the world, and suggests a new model for the resolution of this tension.

The symbol of the Virgin Mary has come almost to epitomize the problems for women who attempt to continue within the Christian tradition. Impossibly pure, suffering nobly, disenfranchised, and sugared with a layer of Victorian sentimentality: both biologically

Introduction

Virgin and Mother. Yet meanings change. The porcelain statue can become a figure of earthy womanhood, Mother of God, autonomous and powerful, who accepts the challenge of bearing a child without any relation to any man. Christian women who are studying their traditions for new interpretations are not helped by secular attempts to dismiss such traditions altogether.

Religious traditions have their own vocabulary for defining the Female. It may not be to women's advantage, but it is there, and it acknowledges the power, albeit negative, of women's cycles of fertility. In secular western culture, however, the physical events of women's lives meet with a resounding silence. Perhaps we are seeing emerge a new paradox, where the voice that breaks the silence is reclaimed from religious, not secular traditions.

This book was born out of the Channel 4 Television series of the same name, and so I would like to thank my friend and colleague Susan Eatwell Conte, with whom the original idea was developed and who produced the series. I would also like to thank Bob Towler at Channel 4 who commissioned it; and the production team.

A group of extraordinary people contributed to the series. Some of them appear in this book, but all of them were immeasurably helpful in developing my thoughts.

In the transition from series to book, Susanna Yager at Channel 4 greatly assisted. Judith Longman at SPCK has been a very supportive and sensitive editor. I would also like to thank the staff of the British Library, Great Russell Street.

Lastly, I would like to thank my parents for making me the Judaeo-Christian hybrid that I am; and my husband Timothy Boon for his support and (not always welcome) criticism. To Tim and to our son Nathaniel this book is dedicated.

NOTES

1 This does depend on denomination and place. Also, the Russian and Greek Orthodox churches tend to take a different view of menstruation.
2 Mary Douglas, *Purity and Danger*. London, Ark, 1984.
3 Penelope Shuttle and Peter Redgrove, *The Wise Wound*. London, Paladin, 1986.

1 Rosemary Radford Ruether

Women's Body and Blood: The Sacred and the Impure

'Anthropologists' study of human societies on this planet [has] revealed the condition of women to be a direct result of their peoples' perception of their mysterious, fearsome, monthly flow of blood.' So declare Janice Delaney, Mary Jane Lupton and Emily Toth, in the preface to their book, *The Curse: A Cultural History of Menstruation*[1]. Most human religions, from tribal to world religions, have treated woman's body, in its gender-specific sexual functions, as impure or polluted and thus to be distanced from sacred spaces and rites dominated by males. Female blood shed in menstruation and childbirth has been the particular focus on this definition of woman as polluted, over against male sacrality.

Such taboos have not entirely disappeared today. Orthodox Judaism continues to teach an elaborate separation of the menstruating woman from contact with the men of her family. Although menstrual taboos and generalized views of women as impure are less explicit in historical Christianity, remnants of such concepts persist even in Western churches.

For example, Swedish Lutheran women have been ordained to the priesthood of their national Church since the late 1950s. Yet a small group of members of this Church, led mostly by male priests, continues to oppose women's ordination, arguing that women, by their very nature, cannot represent Christ. Some of these Lutheran priests also claim that women's bodies are impure and so the presence of a woman at the altar would pollute the sacred rites. One such male priest conducted a ritual of purification of a church after a woman priest had celebrated Mass there.[2]

Roman Catholicism continues officially to oppose the ordination of women, also arguing that woman by her very nature cannot image Christ.[3] Although arguments about women's impurity are not used explicitly in the statements of the Vatican and various national episcopacies against women's ordination, they are implied. The claim that women cannot image Christ is rooted in an Aristotelian-scholastic argument that women, by their very nature, are defective and 'misbegotten'.

According to Aristotle, the male semen provides the formative power that shapes the foetus, mentally and physically. Women provide the 'matter' or 'blood' that is shaped by this male formative power. The male power in procreation is the active power; women's contribution is passive. The generation of a woman comes about when the male formative power fails to shape fully the recalcitrant female 'matter', and so an incomplete being results, lacking in full mental, volitional and physical powers.[4]

Thomas Aquinas and other scholastics appropriated this Aristotelian theory to argue that women are inherently inferior and non-normative. Only the male possesses full or complete human nature. Thus Christ, in order to represent the human, must be male. Only the male, in turn, can represent Christ, the paradigm of perfect humanity united to the Word of God.[5] According to Augustine, women also lack the image of God in themselves, and are related to the divine image only under the male 'who is their head'.[6]

These arguments were originally intended to exclude women from autonomy and leadership, both in the political and in the ecclesiastical realms. Today, with the winning of the vote and civil rights for women, changes which the Catholic church opposed at the time,[7] the secular aspect of this argument of women's inferiority is muted in Catholic pronouncements. It is even claimed that the Catholic Church has always supported women's civil equality[8] (a patent untruth). However, the argument that women do not image Christ (or God) continues to be used to exclude women from ordained leadership in the Church.[9]

Pollution taboos linger in Catholicism even for laywomen. Catholic canon law opposes laywomen and girls performing even semi-sacerdotal roles, such as altar server. Even for roles such as lector, the layman or even the boy is preferred. If there is no suitable male, a female can be employed, with preference for the nun or celibate woman. The sexual woman thus is put at the bottom of a hierarchy of clerical over lay, male over female, celibate over sexual. Should it become necessary to call upon women for such tasks, all women, even the celibate woman, are enjoined to read the Scriptures outside the sanctuary rail. The roots of this injunction lie in the perception of woman as impure and hence to be excluded from the sacred male space.[10]

Another example of lingering pollution taboos in Catholicism lies in the ban on including women in the Holy Thursday ceremony of the washing of the feet. The bishop of Pittsburg officially informed his priests during Holy Week of 1987 that women were not to be included in this ceremony. This same ban was reiterated by Bishop John Donoghue of Charlotte, North Carolina, in February 1989. There were major protests against these bans. Priests in some parishes decided to drop the ceremony altogether, rather than comply with the ban against women's participation.

Although the American Catholic bishops were embarrassed by the uproar, they did not dispute the ruling. As a body they upheld the interpretation of canon law as prohibiting women from this ceremony.[11] The official argument was that this ceremony reflected Jesus' washing of his disciples' feet, all of them males. But since the ceremony symbolizes the rejection of hierarchical status and Jesus' adoption of the servant role, making a male status privilege out of those whose feet can be washed contradicts what most Christians assume to be its message. It is hard to escape the implication that a major source of this taboo is the sense that the priest kneeling down and washing women's 'naked' feet would be somehow both sexual and polluting to the sacred.

These taboos against women as polluting to male sacred space are very ancient. It is not the intention of this brief essay to give a comprehensive history of these ideas and their development in Christianity. But it would be useful to give some brief background of their incorporation by the Christian Church.

In many cultures the girl is secluded from the rest of society during menarche, sometimes for a prolonged period, and is made to undergo rituals of initiation into her new status as a fertile woman that range from brutal to instructive and celebratory. It is also typical of such practices that the menstruating woman withdraws into a separate secluded area or hut in subsequent monthly menses.[12] Since, in many tribal societies, women were either pregnant or nursing during most of their fertile period of life, this monthly menstrual withdrawal did not affect women's lives from month to month as much as it might seem to us today.

Moreover, it is likely that, in many tribal societies, this ability of women to bleed and not die was not seen simply as negative. Menstrual taboos, even in their Jewish expressions, are replete with an ambivalent fusion of the sacred and the taboo. Menstrual blood was seen as powerful and magical. It was seen as having both healing and destructive power. This sense of its power is reflected, even negatively, in the description found in Pliny's *Natural History*.

> Contact with it turns new wine sour, crops touched by it become barren, grafts die, seeds in gardens are dried up, the edge of steel and the gleam of ivory are dulled, hives of bees die, even bronze and iron are at once seized by rust, and a horrible smell fills the air; to taste it drives dogs mad and infects their bites with an incurable poison...[13]

Menstrual blood is seen as debilitating particularly to males and male power; to their sexual, aggressive and spiritual powers. Thus most traditional societies taboo female handling of food to be served to men and also sexual intercourse during this period. The touch of menstrual blood on the male penis is feared as causing impotency or even its rotting away, obvious castration fantasies. Food handled by the menstruating woman will be corrupted, for men. Male aggression in hunting and war is also seen as affected. If the male wants to be potent in these activities, he must avoid the menstruating woman. The notion that the menstruating woman pollutes the sacred spaces of men is the sublimation of these fantasies that the female blood power will render male physio-cultural power null and void.

One cannot help but wonder whether these taboos originally had another meaning. Did they represent a time when women gathered apart from men, experiencing their own primal potency, and sharing their own secrets with one another and with the pubescent girls? Even under the weight of negative male definitions of female bodily processes, there remain hints of its positive aspects for women. Menstruation was a week's holiday for the woman who would provide no services for the males of her family, in cooking, cleaning or sex, during this period. If, as some believe, women living in community tend to synchronize cycles, this would mean that a group of women would retire together. In some African tribes women gather together, apart from men, laughing and enjoying themselves during their time apart.[14]

Anthropological studies, interpreted from the male perspective, typically fail to notice how gender segregation also creates female bonding and shared sense of female power. Women create their own culture, or interpretation of reality, from their own context, a culture that remains invisible and unknown to men.

The result of the male monopoly on public power, however, has resulted in the loss of this female culture. Women themselves are more and more socialized into the male interpretation of these female blood mysteries. Women come to think of themselves as debilitated and polluted, rather than magically powerful, because of their bleeding. For Christianity menstruation becomes the 'curse', the ratification of women's subjugated status as punishment for her primal sin as daughters of the primal woman Eve, who lost paradise for humankind and caused evil to come into the world.

This sense of woman's uncleanness as separating her both from men and from the realm of holiness is developed in the Levitical codes:

> When a woman has a discharge of blood which is her regular discharge from her body, she shall be in her impurity for seven days, and whoever touches her shall be unclean until the evening. And everything upon which she lies during her impurity shall be unclean; everything also upon which she sits shall be unclean. And whoever touches her bed shall wash his clothes and bathe himself in water, and be unclean until the evening. And whoever touches anything upon which she sits shall wash his clothes, and bathe himself in water, and be unclean until the evening; whether it is the bed or anything upon which she sits, when he touches it he shall be unclean until the evening. And if any man lies with her, and her impurity is on him, he shall be unclean seven days; and every bed on which he lies shall be unclean. (Lev. 15.19–24).

The text goes on to make clear that the same elaborate rules of impurity apply to any discharge of blood that occurs to a woman outside of her regular menstruation. The impurity is not confined to the actual time of bleeding, but continues for seven days beyond the last sign of vaginal blood, thus effectively confining women to this state of impurity for twelve to fifteen days of the month. Only after these days can she present herself to the priest for ritual atonement of her impurity:

> But if she is cleansed of her discharge, she shall count for herself seven days, and after that she shall be clean. And on the eighth day she shall take two turtledoves or two young pigeons and bring them to the priest, to the door of the tent of meeting. And the priest shall offer one for a sin offering and the other for a burnt offering; and the priest shall make atonement for her before the Lord for her unclean discharge. Thus you

shall keep the people of Israel separate from their uncleanness, lest they die in their uncleanness by defiling my tabernacle that is in their midst. (Lev. 15.28–31)

The blood discharged by a woman during birthing is also seen as rendering her unclean. A woman who bears a male child is unclean for seven days, plus an additional thirty-three days, to complete the process of purification. If she bears a female child, this period of impurity is doubled to two weeks, plus sixty-six days, a ruling that makes clear that femaleness *per se* is a source of uncleanliness. Here too she must offer a sin offering and a burnt offering as atonement, preferably a young lamb and a turtledove, although a second turtledove can be substituted for the lamb for poor women (Lev. 12.1–8).

Men are also made unclean by bodily emission. The man who has an emission of semen (other than the ejaculation into the woman's vagina) is subjected to the same laws of purification as the menstruating woman (Lev. 15.1–18). But these laws are intended to prevent men from such 'wastage' of seed, and thus define men much less intrinsically than the blood taboos define women *qua* women as unclean.

Biblical Judaism created a series of separations in time and space defined by laws of purity and impurity. The Temple compound, in its fullest development in the time of Herod, became a series of concentric circles of gradated purity. The inner sanctuary or Holy of Holies could be entered only by the High Priest, once a year on the Day of Atonement. In front of the Temple was the court of the priests, to be entered only by the male priestly caste. Surrounding this court was the court of the men of Israel, reserved for non-priestly Jewish males. Then came the court of the women, which men could also enter, but which was as close to the sanctuary as women could come. Outside these courts was the court of the gentiles. Jewish women were excluded from the court of the women during their impurity and fell into the same category of impurity as gentiles.[15]

In her book on Jewish feminist theology, *Standing Again at Sinai*[16], Judith Plaskow has pointed to this paralleling of the impurity of gentiles and the impurity of (Jewish) women in biblical and rabbinic thought. The people of Israel are thought of as a people chosen by God who are to separate themselves from the rest of the peoples of the earth by a series of laws that distinguish the holy time (sabbath) from profane time, clean foods from unclean foods, clean from unclean bodily states and holy from unholy places. Through these discriminations of time, space and substances, they are to make themselves a holy people, set apart from the unholy people and things.

In this scheme of separations of holy from unholy, (Jewish) women are, as it were, the 'gentile within', the unholy half of the holy people. Jewish men make themselves more holy by separating from Jewish women, both to avoid women's impurity and to seek a holy space for prayer and relation to God, defined by the exclusion of the female. This sense that the holiness of God's presence is incompatible with the presence of women is brought out in the story of the giving of the law at Sinai. It is said that the men of Israel are to prepare themselves for three days for this awesome disclosure of God by not going near a woman (Exod. 19.15).

The exclusion of women from this central moment in the history of the 'people' of Israel, when they are made God's holy people, has caused great difficulty for Jewish religious feminists. They have asked if Jewish women have ever really been included in the Jewish covenant. Is the covenant a relation between God and Jewish males, in which Jewish women are included under it, but not as persons who enter into the contract in their own right? If this is the case, then, as Rachel Adler has asked, does there not have to be a 'recovenanting' between Israel and God in order to fully and explicitly include Jewish women?[17] This critical question lies behind Plaskow's title for her book on *Judaism from a Feminist Perspective, Standing Again at Sinai*.

The laws of purity developed in Leviticus were elaborated by the rabbinic teachers, and applied more strictly to relations in the family, as the Temple worship was abolished by the Roman destruction of the second Temple in AD70 (see Leonie Archer's essay in this book). These rules were modified by reform Judaism in modern times and, to a lesser extent, by conservative Judaism, but remain in full force for the orthodox, the group that predominates as the only legitimate expression of Judaism in the present State of Israel. Much of the egalitarianism of the democratic socialist Zionism that shaped the origins of this state has been gradually eroded as the orthodox rabbinates, Ashkenazi and Sephardic, seek to impose the various laws of purity on the public culture of the state of Israel.[18]

Through the Devil's Gateway

Christianity, as it arose as a messianic reform movement within Judaism in the first century AD, had some characteristics of an early reform Judaism. Like modern reform Judaism, it wished to discard laws of purity of time, space and bodily fluids and to focus on the ethical and universalist aspects of the biblical faith. In the Gospels Jesus is presented as violating various laws of sabbath, of cleanliness and of not associating with unclean persons, such as women, sinners and gentiles. These violations of laws of purity and holiness are justified in terms of more fundamental principles, concern for the inner ethical motivations of the person, rather than their external bodily state, and respect for all persons, regardless of gender or ethnicity.

Jesus is portrayed as violating many taboos relating to women. In a story found in all three synoptic Gospels (Mark 5.25–34; Matt. 9.18–26; Luke 8.40–56) he heals a woman who has been unclean for many years because of a flow of blood. This woman violates the taboo of not touching any man when in a state of impurity by secretly touching his garment, hoping thereby to heal herself. Jesus experiences her touch as a flow of healing power from himself. Turning and seeing her, he affirms her deed as an act of faith: 'Daughter, your faith has made you well; go in peace and be healed of your disease.'

In a story in Luke 13.10–17 Jesus violates the taboo against healing on the sabbath by healing a woman who has been bent over for many years, justifying this on the grounds that it is even more urgent to help a fellow human being, a woman, than to rescue an animal that has fallen into a ditch (an exception allowed under the law). Jesus is also pictured as consorting with women tabooed because of their sinful or their gentile status or the combination of the two, such as the healing of the daughter of the Syrophoenician woman (Matt. 15.21–8; Mark 7.24–30), the commissioning to preach of the much-married Samaritan woman (John 4.7–42); the acceptance of the ointment of blessing from the sinful woman (Luke 7.36–50), and the close association with Mary Magdalene, a woman described as having been healed by him from seven demons (probably a reference to convulsive disease: Luke 8.1–3).[19]

This tradition that the redemption brought by Christ has abolished laws of purity that distinguished between clean and unclean animals, clean and unclean foods, clean and unclean people (Jew and gentile) and clean and unclean physical states (women during menstruation) restrained Christianity for several centuries from applying laws of impurity to women. The Church Fathers of the first three centuries affirmed that all of the natural world was essentially and equally good. It blasphemed God's goodness to declare that one day, the seventh, was holier than the other six (the Christian Sunday was seen as the eighth day, pointing beyond time to eternity); that some food or animals were clean and others unclean; that some nations were less God's children than others, or that a natural function, such as menstruation, made women unholy and hence unfit for contact with God.[20]

However, this impulse to abolish distinctions of holiness within a universal community of creation was deeply contradicted by an opposite influence on Christianity from gnosticism which viewed the whole material creation, and especially sexuality, as a realm of fallenness separated from God. Female sexuality and reproduction were seen particularly as representative of the mortality that separates us from the eternal and binds us to temporal corruptible life. This ascetic direction of Christianity exalted the celibate, both male and female, who abstained from both sex and reproduction and devoted themselves entirely to the coming new age that will transcend the corruptible world of birth and death.[21]

In its earliest impulses celibacy was egalitarian and even subversive of patriarchal family relationships. The celibate woman was seen as having been freed from the 'curse of Eve', to bear children in sorrow and to be under the domination of the male. Redeemed by Christ into a renewed virginal state, she has been restored to her original spiritual equality and autonomy.[22] Early Christian popular ascetic literature abounds with stories of women who reject the fiancés imposed on them by their families, and even reject their husbands. Opting for Christian celibacy, they leave home, travel about, sometimes dressed as males, conquer natural and human adversaries and are affirmed by their male apostle-mentors as teachers.[23]

But by the late first century, a patriarchal family-oriented Christianity began to counteract and repress this anti-familial and egalitarian construction of celibacy. The repeated assertions in the New Testament that 'wives should obey their husbands' and that women will be saved by childbearing, reflect the war of familial, patriarchal Christianity against egalitarian, celibate Christianity. By the mid-fourth century the patriarchal line of Church leadership began to fuse with a male construction of celibacy that defined it both as avoidance of contact with women as the source of sin and as a source of power over inferior married people. Celibacy, originally a voluntary charism, became a requirement for ordination, although it would not be until the eleventh century that this law would be fully imposed on the Latin Church.[24]

The fusion of patriarchal male dominance, clerical hierarchy and celibacy, as the norm for the ordained, reshaped the definition of celibacy as an expression of superior holiness. The holiness of celibacy comes to be identified with the holiness of the sacramental cult. The priest must be celibate in order to purify himself for the handling of the sacred in the sacrament. This concept of priesthood allowed a revival of the purity taboos associated with the Temple cult and priesthood of the Hebrew Bible. The priest avoids contact with sexuality and women in order to make himself holy and fit for handling the sacred. Women, by contrast, even celibate women, are unholy. They are, by their very female nature, unfit to enter the sacred space of the altar or handle its sacred elements.

Canon Law in Western Christianity from the sixth to ninth centuries elaborated sexual taboos designed to segregate women as unclean from sacred space, persons and things. Even the celibate woman who cleans the altar linens, vestments and vessels, must cover her hands when she handles these sacred things, lest she pollute them by her touch. All women *qua* women should be strictly excluded from entering the sanctuary where the priest stands at the altar.[25] It is during this period that various decrees and opinions of church leaders advise women to abstain from the Eucharist and even to refrain from entering the church altogether when they are menstruating. The woman recently delivered of child is given a Christian version of the rite of purification of Leviticus 12.[26]

These kinds of purity laws have gradually faded from explicit reference in modern Western Christianity. They survive today as an echo, an implicit feeling, rather than an acknowledged principle. This feeling is stronger in the priestly or cultic traditions, than in de-sacramentalized Protestantism. Roman Catholicism preserves clear remnants of the medieval canonical teaching in its exclusion of women from the sanctuary as altar servers, or even as participants in the rite of footwashing. Swedish Lutheranism, with its strong medieval roots, also has not forgotten such ideas entirely.

In Roman Catholicism male hierarchy is reinforced by the hierarchy of the celibate over the sexual, making the sexual female the bottom of its ladder of holiness. But even in a Lutheranism which has had married priests for four centuries, the notion that the mere presence of a woman acting as priest pollutes the sanctuary can still be a powerful belief.

Women in Christianity today stand at the crossroads between two directions. One direction seeks to neutralize gender differences. Femaleness, including female bodily states, such as menstruation, pregnancy and lactation, are defined as making no difference to women's basic abilities. Studies show that women workers on the average lose no more work hours because of illness than do men. It is therefore untrue that menstruation is a disability that inordinately incapacitates women. Men too have monthly psychic rhythms. Women, in the pre-menstrual phase, may even experience enhanced aggressiveness and clarity of thought.[27] The claim that women can never be in positions of public responsibility because of their 'raging hormonal imbalances' is refuted.[28]

This type of equality, however, is based on the male norm. Women seek to prove that they can perform equally with men, without, however, any allowances for those things that make them different, both physiologically and socially. The result is that women typically become 'equal' by having to do more, to stretch themselves to work as hard as a man, even when experiencing bodily processes that a male has never experienced. They also work the same hours, only to rush off afterwards to do child care, shopping, cooking and cleaning tasks from which men are exempt.

In the religious realm, there is also an effort to make women 'equal' by neutralization of sexual symbolism. A woman priest will dress in the same collar, robes and vestments as the male. She will learn to preach and do the liturgy in the same way as he. There is an avoidance of recognizing the way her mere presence as a female in the Christian 'sacred spaces' changes the symbolic and psychic dynamics of relationship to the holy. Liberal Christians laugh at the frightened question of traditionalists: 'What if she were pregnant at the altar?'

What indeed if she is pregnant at the altar? What difference does this make? The issue is not that she might faint or be incapable of carrying through her role of blessing bread and wine and distributing it, then wiping out the sacred vessels, for these are not exactly arduous tasks! The real issue is that the power of the female to gestate is brought back into symbolic conjunction with the generation of the divine presence, a conjunction excluded by patriarchal religion for four millennia. A profound psychical revolution might erupt from this experience of the pregnant female as priest.

Some Christian women are dissatisfied with this route to equality through male generic neutrality. This path to 'equality' always puts women in a double bind, seeking to be twice as good, yet always failing to be adequate. Although the problem may not always be clearly articulated, these women are seeking alternative rituals that affirm female distinctiveness as a source of sacrality. The woman-church movement is one expression of this impulse to reaffirm the sacrality of female distinctiveness.

In my book, *Woman-church: Theology and Practice of Feminist Liturgical Communities*[29], the female life-cycle is affirmed as a locus of sacred time. There is exploration of rituals for childbirth, for menarche or first menstruation, for monthly menstruation and for menopause. Some of these rituals draw upon the creative work of Jewish feminist ritualists who are reclaiming traditional practices, like the monthly ritual bath and the new moon celebration, as distinctive and positive rituals for women that celebrate female bodily processes.[30]

There are also liturgies in this book that focus on specific kinds of sexual violence to women and the need for healing from sexual violence. Healing from incest violation, from rape and from wife battering name female experiences of violence that remain unmentionable in patriarchal religion. The divine has long been made an intimate participant in male experiences of violence, in war and in political martyrdom. But the female body tortured by sexual violence has been the object of pornography, not sacrament. That God might enter the pain of the beaten or raped woman, or be privy both to that pain and the power of healing from that pain, is a revelatory insight.[31]

The path of equality through androcentric neutralization and the reaffirmation of female sacrality will not combine in an easy synthesis. Patriarchal religion is built on many millennia of repressed fear of the power of female bodily processes. Any effort to admit the female in her explicit femaleness, as one who menstruates, gestates and lactates, will create psychic time-bombs that may explode with incalculable force. One can expect cries of 'witchcraft', 'blasphemy', 'sacrilege' and 'idolatry' to be directed against those who seek to resacralize the female body. Such cries should not cause feminist liturgists to retreat in fear. Rather they alert us to just how powerful female potency really is in our collective psyches, despite, and even because of, its long repression.

NOTES

1. Janice Delaney, Mary Jane Lupton and Emily Toth, *The Curse: A Cultural History of Menstruation*. Chicago, University of Illinois Press, 1988.
2. This incident took place in the diocese of Lund, Sweden and was recounted to me by Lutheran women priests Ulla Carin Holm and Anna Carin Hammer during my stay there in the fall of 1984.
3. 'Declaration on the Question of the Admission of Women to the Ministerial Priesthood', Vatican, Congregation for the Doctrine of the Faith, 15 October 1976 (37).
4. Aristotle, *The Generation of Animals*, 729b, 738b, 737a and 775a.
5. Thomas Aquinas, *Summa Theologica*, Q85, arts 1–6.
6. Augustine, *On the Trinity*, 7,7,10.
7. In the first decades of the twentieth century the American Catholic bishops opposed women's suffrage, echoing the hostility of the papacy to women's civil rights: see Rosemary Radford Ruether, *Contemporary Roman Catholicism: Crises and Challenges*. Kansas City, Sheed and Ward, 1987, pp.36–7.
8. This argument that the Church has always supported women's equality in society is made in the opening sections of the Vatican 'Declaration on the Question of the Admission of Women to the Ministerial Priesthood' (1976) in an effort to separate women's civil rights from the question of ordination.
9. This argument is repeated in the pastoral of the American Catholic bishops, 'Partners in the Mystery of Redemption: A Pastoral Response to Women's Concerns for Church and Society', Washington DC, NCCB, April 1988, and also in the Apostolic Letter issued by Pope John Paul II, *Mulieris Dignitatem* (The Dignity and Vocation of Women), 31 September 1988.
10. For the canonical basis of this argument, see John M. Huels, *Disputed Questions in the Liturgy Today* (Chicago, Liturgy Training Institute, 1988), pp. 27–37.
11. See *National Catholic Reporter*, 24 February 1989, pp. 1,6.
12. See Delaney, *et al.*, *The Curse*, pp. 7–17.

13 Pliny, *Natural History*, trans. H. Rackham (Cambridge MA, Harvard University Press, 1942), p. 87.
14 Marjorie Shostak, *Nisa: The Life and Words of a !Kung Woman*. Cambridge MA, Harvard University Press, 1981.
15 Josephus, *Against Apion*, bk. II, 102–4.
16 San Francisco, Harper and Row, 1990.
17 See Rachel Adler, 'Can Jewish Women Re-Covenant?', unpublished manuscript.
18 Norman L. Zucker, *The Coming Crisis in Israel: Private Faith and Public Policy*. Cambridge MA, MIT Press, 1973; also Ian Lustick, *For the Land and the Lord: Jewish Fundamentalism in Israel*. New York, Council on Foreign Relations, 1988.
19 Mary Magdalene has been misinterpreted as a forgiven sinner and 'ex-prostitute' by the Christian tradition, based on a mistaken conflation of the texts of Mark 14.3–9, Luke 7.36–50, and John 12.1–8, none of which refer to Mary Magdalene. The reference to Mary Magdalene as having been healed of seven devils cannot be interpreted as a former sinful state of life, since, in the Gospels, healing from demon possession is not a reference to personal sin, but to convulsive disease. See Rosemary Radford Ruether, *Womanguides: Readings Toward a Feminist Theology* (Boston, Beacon Press, 1985), pp. 177–8.
20 The early Christian rejection of distinctions between clean and unclean peoples and animals is developed in Peter's dream in Acts 10.9–36. Among the Church Fathers, the idea that all natural things, days, foods and animals, are good since God created a good creation, is often developed in polemics against Jewish laws of sabbath and kosher; i.e. Novatian, *De Cibis Iudaicis*. In the sixth century Pope Gregory I of Rome replied to an inquiry from Augustine, Bishop of Canterbury, concerning whether women should be excluded from communion and from entering the church during their menstrual period. The Pope replied that women should not be barred from church or communion during those times, because the monthly courses of women are not a fault of women, but are caused by nature; see Bede, *History of the English Church and People* (Baltimore, Penguin, n.d.), pp. 76–81.
21 Rosemary Radford Ruether, 'Misogynism and Virginal Feminism In the Fathers of the Church', in Rosemary Radford Ruether, ed., *Religion and Sexism: Images of Women in the Jewish and Christian Traditions* (New York, Simon and Schuster, 1974), pp. 150–83.
22 Rosemary Radford Ruether, 'Asceticism and Feminism: Strange Bedfellows?', in *Sex and God: Some Varieties of Women's Religious Experience*, Linda Hurcombe (ed.), (London, Routledge and Kegan Paul, 1987), pp. 229–50.
23 This celebration of the independence of the ascetic woman is found especially in the apocryphal acts, which some scholars have suggested is a women's literature: see Steven Davies, *The Revolt of the Widows: The Social World of the Apocryphal Acts*. Southern Illinois University Press, 1980.

24 The first effort to mandate celibacy for the clergy is found in the AD 300 Spanish Council of Elvira. The canons of this Council are replete with hostility to women and to sexuality as sin: see Samuel Laeuchli, *Power and Sexuality: The Emergence of Canon Law at the Council of Elvira*. Philadelphia, Temple University Press, 1972.
25 This theme has been developed particularly in Susan Wemple, *Women in Frankish Society: Marriage and the Cloister, 500–900 AD*. Philadelphia, University of Pennsylvania Press, 1983.
26 Modern Christian liturgical books have either dropped the ceremony of the 'churching of women' or else tried to conceal its purificatory meaning by describing it as a celebration of childbirth. For its historical development, see C.J. Cuming, 'The Churching of Women', in J.D. Davies (ed.), *New Westminster Dictionary of Liturgy and Worship*, (Philadelphia, Westminster, 1986), pp. 175–6.
27 See Delaney, *et al.*, *The Curse*, pp. 54–66 and 267–73.
28 This phrase was used by Dr Edgard Berman, Democratic Party leader, who employed it, in 1970, to claim that women are unfit for national leadership: see Delaney et al, *The Curse*, p. 55.
29 San Francisco, Harper and Row, 1988.
30 See Rachel Adler, 'Tumah and Taharah: Ends and Beginnings' and Arlene Agus, 'This Month is for You: Observing Rosh Hodesh as a Woman's Holiday', in Elizabeth Koltun (ed.), *The Jewish Woman* (New York, Schocken, 1976), pp. 63–71 and 84–93.
31 In a class on violence to women taught in Chicago in 1984 a woman student described her experience of being raped and how the image of Christ as a crucified woman appeared to her as she lay on the ground after this experience, allowing her to believe that God 'knew what it was like to be a woman who had been raped'.

2 Leonie J. Archer

'In thy blood live': Gender and Ritual in the Judaeo-Christian tradition

> Thus saith the Lord God unto Jerusalem . . . In the day that thou wast born thy navel wast not cut, neither wast thou washed in water for cleansing; thou wast not salted at all, nor swaddled at all. No eye pitied thee, to do any of these things unto thee; but thou wast cast out in the open field in the loathsomeness of thy person . . . And when I passed by thee and saw thee wallowing in thy blood, I said unto thee: in thy blood live . . . I swore unto thee, and entered into a covenant with thee, and thou becamest mine. Then washed I thee with water; yea, I cleansed away thy blood from thee and I anointed thee with oil. (Ezek. 16.3–6, 8–9)

It is evident from even the most cursory reading of the Hebrew Bible, in particular the Five Books of Moses (the Pentateuch), that blood, mentioned in this passage several times and with various significances, played an all-important role in the ancient Jewish belief system. In the narratives, descriptions of killing are specifically and explicitly couched in terms of the shedding of another person's blood, whilst acts of lawful vengeance for clan murder are similarly spoken of in terms of effecting an expiation by blood (Lev. 20.9,11,12,13,etc.; Num. 35.19ff); one of the earliest attested acts of faith centred upon the near sacrifice of a human being (Isaac, son of Abraham), replaced at the last moment by a substitute ram which was given as a burnt-offering (Gen. 22); and the first redemption of the embryonic nation Israel involved the smearing of the blood of the Passover lamb on the doorposts and lintels of the Hebrews' homes in Egypt as a sign to the Angel of Death to leave them in safety (Exod. 12.7,13,23).

In the law, particularly that concerned with cultic activity, blood is all-pervasive. The consecration of the High Priest to his office, the highest and most sacred in the nation, was effected by sprinkling his garments and daubing his right ear, thumb and foot with the blood of a sacrificed animal (Exod. 29.20–21; Lev.

8.22–24, 30); in sacrificial ritual generally, the main activity of the Temple at Jerusalem, the principal feature was the dashing of the blood of animals on the horns of the altar and on the floor of the sanctuary (Exod. 29; Lev. *passim*; Num. 18–19, 28–9). Such cultic shedding of blood was regarded as the means of connecting with the Godhead, and animals were brought to the priests for sacrifice as sin- and thank-offerings, for purging ritual impurity, covenanting and redemption of both the individual and the nation as a whole (Lev. *passim*; Num. 6,7,8,15,28–29). The consumption of blood by humans was absolutely forbidden for, as Leviticus 17.11 declared, '... the life of the flesh is in the blood'. Whilst humans could eat meat, they could only do so after careful selection and preparation of the animal (Lev. 11, 17.10ff). The blood always belonged to God, for 'I have given it to you upon the altar to make atonement for your souls ... whosoever eateth any manner of blood, I will set my face against that soul ... and will cut him off from among his people' (Lev. 17.10–11). The ceremonial accoutrements which were an essential accompaniment to the sacrificial procedure were also all of significant colour (scarlet wool, hyssop, cedar wood – Exod. 25.4,14; 26.1,31,36; 28.5ff; 35.23 – 6; 39.1–5,22–9; Lev. 14.6, etc.), and the most important sacrifice of the year was that of the red heifer (Num. 19).

That a deep-seated and all-embracing blood taboo unquestionably lay at the heart of so much of Jewish belief and ritual practice is clearly evidenced by the later (Christian) book of Hebrews which saw fit to characterize Judaism specifically as a covenant of blood, sanctified, purified and redeemed by the blood of cultic sacrifice:

> Even the first covenant was not ratified without blood. For when every commandment of the law had been declared by Moses to all the people, he took the blood of calves and goats, with water and scarlet wool and hyssop, and sprinkled both the book itself and all the people, saying, 'This is the blood of the covenant which God commanded you.' And in the same way he sprinkled with the blood both the tent and all the vessels used in worship. Indeed, under the law almost everything is purified with blood, and without the shedding of blood there is no forgiveness of sins. (Heb. 9.18–22).

The point of interest from all of these examples is not only the obvious centrality of blood to Jewish ritual thought and practice, but also the fact that virtually all of the significant references to blood derive from the book of Leviticus and other chronologically allied strands of the Old Testament. The Bible has long been recognized as a composite work spanning many centuries, not some kind of monolithic whole, and whilst opinions differ widely as to the precise dating (and methods of dating) of its constituent parts, it remains the case that a book, or indeed a chapter, may lie in the received text next to a verse or chapter some several centuries removed in compositional/redactional terms from its neighbour. All of the references given above come from what is called the Priestly strand ('P') and as such they are to be dated to around the time of the Jews' exile to Babylon in the sixth century BC – that is, according to the still widely accepted dating of this biblical strand within the source-critical school of thought (though it must also be said that my own arguments as developed in this essay and elsewhere independently point to the exile as the time when these blood concerns and rituals would first have emerged).[1]

Additionally, and of equal significance, is the fact that within the overall blood taboo context there seems to have been a clear and hierarchical distinction made between male blood and female blood. This may be seen not only from a detailed breakdown of the sacrificial prescriptions in terms of the sex of the victim chosen for particular occasions, but more especially from an analysis of two other rituals which appeared on the scene at the same time: covenantal (male) circumcision and the regulations surrounding menstruation and childbirth.[2] Both of these involved a flow of blood, the one positively valued, the other negatively, and both had profound resonances for men's and women's involvement (or non-involvement) in public religion. It is these two rituals which will be the main focus of this essay, but before turning to their specific analysis a few more words need to be said about the general blood context and the male–female hierarchy at work within it.

Within the sacrificial procedure, the prescription was always to select male victims for the more important occasions. Thus, the cult offerings for all the major feasts, including the sabbath, new moon and Passover, were all male animals (Num. 28); the sin-offering of a priest had to be an unblemished bullock (Lev. 4.2ff, 9.3, 16.6ff); similarly sacrifice to atone for the guilt of the nation was also a bullock (*idem*; cf. Num. 15.22ff); the sin-offering of a ruler was a male goat without blemish (Lev. 4.22ff), whilst any guilt-offering for sin 'through error in the holy things of the Lord' was an unblemished ram (Lev. 5.14ff). In all of these instances the animal's blood was daubed on the altar, the fat burned, and the meat of the carcass divided between the sacrificing priest and the offerer for consumption. In cases of individual atonement a whole burnt-offering of a male victim was made (Lev. 1.3ff). Female animals were used only for the less significant peace-offerings when animals of either sex could be sacrificed (Lev. 3.1ff) and for the sin or guilt-offering of a commoner as opposed to that of a priest or ruler (Lev. 4.27ff; cf. Num. 15.27f). The only exception to this clear male–female hierarchy was the occasion of the ceremony of the red heifer when a female was slaughtered for atonement and purification (Num. 19). Significantly, however, this ritual was not allowed to take place within the sacred precincts: the animal was burned whole 'outside the camp', its blood was not offered at the altar but burned along with the carcass, and the officiating priest was required to cleanse himself after the sacrifice.

The fact that there was a clear male–female hierarchy at work within the sacrificial procedure was not unknown to or unappreciated by the ancients. That is, the material presented is not some kind of *post hoc* analysis imposed upon the texts in the light of present-day concerns, removed from the ancients' own understanding of the laws in their original context. Far from it. The first century AD Jewish philosopher Philo, commenting upon the sin-offering prescriptions of Leviticus 4, wrote:

> ... we have several divisions [of sacrifice], both according to the persons concerned and the kinds of victim. As to the persons, the High Priest is distinguished from the whole nation, and the rulers ... from the mass of the common people ... The sins of the High Priest and those of the whole nation are purged with an animal of the same value: in both cases it is directed that a male calf should be brought. For the sins of the ruler one of less value is ordered, though this too is a male, namely a he-goat; for the sins of the commoner, one still more inferior in kind, a female offering instead of a male, that is, a she-goat. For it was proper that in matters of sacrifice the ruler should fare better than the commoner and the nation than the ruler, since the whole should always be superior to the part ...[3]

And with regard to the most sacred sacrifice, the whole burnt-offering, Philo analyses the choice of victim in the following way:

> ... the victim of the whole burnt-offering is a male because the male is more complete, more dominant than the female, closer akin to causal activity, for the female is incomplete and in subjection and belongs to

the category of the passive rather than the active. So too with the two ingredients which constitute our life principle, the rational and the irrational; the rational which belongs to mind and reason is of the masculine gender, the irrational, the province of sense, is of the feminine. Mind belongs to a genus wholly superior to sense as man is to woman; unblemished and purged . . . it is itself the most religious of sacrifices and its whole being is highly pleasing to God.[4]

Bearing Philo's words in mind – in particular his characterization of the male as active/causal and the female as passive – we shall now turn to the main focus of this essay, that is, an examination of the rituals of circumcision and menstrual taboo.

As was noted above and as I shall explore in further detail below, both of these involved a flow of blood – the one positively valued, the other negatively, and both had profound resonances for the involvement or non-involvement of men and women in public religion. Whilst the two rituals are not normally linked together, it does seem from close examination that they are connected and that they are, in analytical terms, in fact opposite sides of the same coin. They deserve our attention not only because of their clear male–female: superior–inferior blood differentiation, but also because, of all the other blood rituals of covenanting, purifying and cleansing discussed above, only they survived the destruction of the Jerusalem Temple in AD 70 to remain rites central to the Judaism of today, with the same religious consequences for men and women as in the ancient world.

The way in which I wish to approach the subject and discuss the notion of gendered blood, as it were, in these two rituals is by means of a socially constructed opposition between culture and nature – circumcision being deemed the work of (superior) culture and menstruation the functioning of (inferior) nature. The nature-versus-culture model of analysis was first developed within anthropology to help account for the universal subordination or secondary status of women in all societies at all times.[5] Basically, the projected dichotomy of the model rests on the assumption that every society recognizes a distinction between culture and nature, with ritual being the outer manifestation or expression of this recognition and representing culture's need to regulate and control the passive functioning of its opposite, nature – 'nature' itself, of course, being a construct of 'culture'. Regarding the social differentiation between the sexes, this conceptual schematization *can* result (and I stress that this is just one possibility, and one which admirably serves the needs of patriarchy) in women being perceived as closer to nature in consequence of the biological facts of childbirth and menstruation (or rather, a particular cultural interpretation thereof), whilst men, who are deemed to lack such a cycle of visible creativity (and who have other aspects of their own equally natural physiology denied), are placed within the realm of culture, manipulating their own social and political existence, and transcending the passive forces of nature. Culture, and therefore male activity within this scheme of thought, are consequently seen as superior to nature and female passivity. It must be emphasized, however, that this particular elaboration of the nature–culture split is, of course, also itself a complex social construct and one which as I said serves patriarchal needs in various ways. The split could have gone in a different direction with different characterizations and emphases within the overall framework. To use the nature–culture dichotomy for a greater understanding of a particular situation is not therefore to promote principles of immutable (socio-) biological determinism.[6] Such then, in extremely broad terms, is the essence of the nature–culture opposition, an opposition which, as I hope to show, provides one clue as to the perceived gender differentials in blood within Judaism and which may be of help in establishing an (oppositional) link between circumcision and menstrual taboo.

Before turning to the specifics of our analysis of the blood taboo in terms of a nature–culture opposition, however, it will be necessary first to sketch in a general historical picture of the changes which occurred in the religious and social ordering of the Jewish community in the centuries surrounding the exile, the time when these rituals, at least in their final form (see below), first emerged. The need for such a sketch is obvious when one recalls that ritual and ritualistic ideas can make sense only when taken in reference to a total structure of thought and system of social and historical reality (most of which I shall, of course, be able only to touch on here). They do not spring from a vacuum or according to some arbitrary whim of the people and legislators, but have their origins in the human need to control and order existence. The way in which ritual develops – or rather is developed – and the characteristics which it assumes, reflect the ordering and preoccupations peculiar to a society. Thus it is essential that we keep in mind that notions which may now seem 'normal' and 'natural' are in fact, as with most things, social and cultural constructs determined by a complex of reasons and situations.

Given that the rituals of circumcision and menstrual taboo, like the other blood rituals, would appear to have derived at least in their final form from the trauma of the exile to Babylon and the consequent restructuring of the Jewish community, we shall need to start our historical survey some centuries further back in time in order to locate and appreciate the profound changes which occurred in and around the sixth century BC. The survey will focus on religious and social development and will be taken largely from the woman's perspective.

From the early chronological strands of the Old Testament, it is apparent that women in the pre-exilic period of Hebrew history enjoyed a certain active involvement in the nation's religious affairs.[7] In the biblical narratives they appear as singers and dancers (see for example, Exod. 15.20–21; Judg. 21.21; Jer. 31.4; Ps. 68.12, 24–5), prophetesses (e.g. Judg. 4.4f; 2 Sam. 20.16f; 2 Kings 22.14f), sacred prostitutes and in other cultic capacities (e.g. Gen. 38; Exod. 38.8; 1 Sam. 2.22; Hos. 4.13–14). Significantly, however, the period to which these texts refer was one in which that rigid monotheism so characteristic of later Judaism had not as yet developed. Then polytheistic belief and worship flourished and shrines to the various deities, which included a number of goddesses, dotted the countryside of Palestine (e.g. Judg. 3.7; 1 Kings 11.5f, 15.13; 2 Kings 23.7; Jer. 7.18, 44.15f). In the course of time, however, the monotheistic principle began to assert itself, and for a complex of reasons not within the scope of this essay, the god Yahweh was elevated to a position of supremacy over all other deities. With this rise to power of a single male deity and the concomitant lessening in status of the other members of the Israelite pantheon (especially its female members), the role played by women in public religion began to diminish. The first step in that direction was taken when the early Hebrew legislators forbade the practice of sacred prostitution, this ritual being fundamental to the non-Yahwistic cults and also one in which women played a central role (Deut. 23.17–18; cf. 1 Kings 15.12; 2 Kings 23.7). Women were further removed from cultic activity when the Yahwists forced the abolition of all ritual shrines in Palestine and centralized worship at the Temple in Jerusalem, a move which was again designed to rid the land of undesirable cults (cf. 1 Kings 6ff).

At this central sanctuary there was no place for female officiants as the Temple's affairs were regarded as the sole responsibility of an organized, hereditary male priesthood dedicated to the service of Yahweh. But despite all efforts, worship of the old gods and goddesses continued throughout the land of Israel and even on occasion at the Temple of Jerusalem itself – as evidenced by the books of Kings and Chronicles, which refer to events of the seventh and sixth centuries. Ironically, Yahweh's final victory came with the destruction of the Temple at the hands of the Babylonians in 587 BC. For generations prior to this calamity the custodians and promoters of Yahweh – that is, the now canonized Prophets of Israel – had been warning the people that if they did not abandon their syncretistic ways, the wrath of the one true God would descend upon them. For the people as a whole, therefore, the destruction of the Temple and the exile to Babylon came to be viewed as a dramatic realization of these doom prophecies, and proof of the absolute power of the jealous God Yahweh, and – harnessing these concepts to their own pragmatic ends – the exiles set about ridding themselves of all impurity in an effort to regain his favour. To this end all records of the past were zealously preserved and older, more primitive legal traditions extensively reworked and edited in the light of developing concepts and attitudes – most of which would seem to have been the direct result of the community's change in circumstances and new needs for order and social cohesion.[8] Of particular significance and far-reaching consequence to the lives of women was the exilic legislators' obsession with ritual cleanness[9] – and in order to understand the full import of this statement, I shall momentarily have to digress from our historical outline and spend a little time analysing the reasons for the legislators' obsession and its impact.

Remembering that we are here dealing with a community first in exile and then returned to an impoverished and divided land (i.e. Palestine towards the end of the sixth and in the course of the fifth centuries BC),[10] it is significant that the principal concern of the Priestly Code (the code with which we are primarily concerned, see p. 24 above) was with the laws of *kashrut*, pollutions from secretions of various bodily orifices, and, as we have seen above, legislation about the cult and priesthood.[11] This concern for purity and order – for that is what the legislation is about – both reflected society's concern for its own racial integrity and social cohesion, and in turn served to promote them. As Mary Douglas writes, 'The idea of society is a powerful image . . . This image has form; it has external boundaries, margins, structure . . . For symbols of society any human experience of structure, margins, or boundaries is ready to hand.'[12] And again, '. . . ideas about separating, purifying, demarcating and punishing transgressions have as their main function to impose system on an inherently untidy experience. It is only by exaggerating the difference between within and without, above and below, male and female, with and against, that a semblance of order is created.'[13] So, for example, the laws of *kashrut*, whilst serving an obvious pragmatic purpose of separating and distinguishing the Jews from their neighbours, and guarding against assimilation, also served to affirm the selected symbolic system, the abomination and avoidance of crawling things being the negative side of the pattern of things approved and a function of the ordering of society.[14] Similarly, the concern for the pollution of and from bodily secretions on a practical level worked to promote the integrity and productivity (in human terms) of the family unit – a matter of prime importance for a group concerned for its very existence and reproduction – whilst on a symbolic level, the exiles' concentration upon the unity, purity and integrity of the physical body well reflected their larger concern for the threatened boundaries of the body politic. The overt rationale behind the new prescriptions was the desire to create a people which was truly holy to God.[15]

Whilst the laws of ritual purity were directed at both men and women,[16] women – in order to promote practical, patriarchal socio-economic concerns – were particularly affected.[17] Central to the legislators' notions of purity was an all-pervasive blood taboo which, as has been demonstrated above, embraced foodstuffs, sacrificial victims, humans, etc., and very definitely separated out the male from the female. The fact that, unlike men, women's periods of bodily emission followed a regular and extended (i.e. several days at a time) cycle meant that they were declared unclean for a large part of their lives (for details see below). Great attention was paid to the pollution which resulted from contact with them during these periods, with vital purification rituals being prescribed to avert the danger to both individuals and community (in particular, the *male religious community*, see below) and restrictions imposed on their movement, particularly with regard to access to the cult, during their times of uncleanness. For, to take just one aspect of this notion of danger, just as crawling things could be seen as the negative side of things approved, so the flow of female blood, again in symbolic terms, could be seen as the negative side of the ideal concept of society as whole and self-contained.[18] In other words, whilst necessary to the system on both practical and symbolic levels, and a strengthening factor to the positive definition, it remained also an offence to the ideal, marginal to the correct order, and therefore dangerous.

It was also of course a source of female power by virtue of the fact that anything that threatens also wields power – a theme which has often been picked by other contributors to this volume. Female danger/power also rested on teh fact that women occupied structurally marginal positions (i.e. neither fully inside nor outside the system, not wholly nature nor culture) and on the fact that society placed them in interstructural roles (as wives and daughters) with respect to alliance-making and linking disparate power groups. Although officially accorded little or no power, it could be argued that women's culturally ambiguous position within Hebrew patriarchy resulted in a type of informal sub-structural power dynamic which in turn regenerated the culturally constructed fear of women necessary to patriarchal interests and explicit power concerns.[19] One aspect of this fear was the way in which the new notion of female impurity rapidly made inroads into the popular imagination, with the result that women came to be seen as a constant stumbling block to man's improvement, a blight on the possibility of his attaining the now required (i.e. post-exilic) standard of personal purity. Thus, in the fourth century, Job:

> Man that is born of woman is of few days and full of trouble ... Who can bring a clean thing out of an unclean? ... What is man that he should be clean? And he that is born of woman that he should be righteous? (Job 14.1;4 15.14)

It was an easy step from this type of attitude to regard women as the source of all evil in the world, and that indeed is what happened in the exile and beyond when there emerged the concept of the Evil Woman, of wickedness personified in female form. Such developments and analysis of the inter/sub structural power dynamic are however the concern of another paper ...[20]

Returning to our historical outline and intimately connected with this new notion of female impurity, was the development of an increased rigidity in attitude toward and definition of function within the family group – something which had gradually been happening before the sixth century but which was accelerated and refined by the experience of the exile.[21] Together with moves towards greater urbanization; more complex economic systems; shifts in societal and familial structure (in particular the movement away from the earlier extended family unit to the nucleated one),[22] there developed the situation whereby the woman's role was placed firmly and almost exclusively in the private sphere of activity as wife, mother and homemaker (a removal encouraged by the purity laws), whilst that of the man was located in the public sphere as worker and family supporter, and active participant in social, political and religious affairs (see, for example, Prov. 31.10ff). This sharp differentiation, and the various impulses and societal shifts which encouraged it (which unfortunately we do not have time to go into here) was quite different from the situation which pertained in earlier Hebrew history. In religious terms, these two exilic and post-exilic developments – i.e. the concentration upon ritual purity and the sharp differentiation in male – female social function – were to have far-reaching consequences for women. Henceforth they were denied access to active participation in the public cult and (by implication of the biblical text which concentrated upon male activity) deemed exempt from the obligation to fulfil many of the commandments – a loaded exemption given the fact that Judaism by this time was already very much a religion of performance, moving towards being a religion dominated by a plethora of commandments governing virtually every aspect of daily existence.[23] This implication was later firmed up by the Sages of the Second Commonwealth to become a fully-fledged rabbinic declaration of exemption embracing nearly all of the positive commandments whose fulfilment depended upon a specific time of the day or year – an exemption which rapidly came to be viewed in terms of actual exclusion (*Kidd.* 1.7; cf. *Sot.* 21a). So, for example, women were under no obligation to circumcise their sons (*Kidd.* 1.7, a point of some significance in the context of this essay, and one to which I shall return later), or take them to the Temple for the ritual redemption of the first-born (*idem*); they were exempt from making the thrice-yearly pilgrimage to Jerusalem at the feasts of Passover, Pentecost and Tabernacles (*Hag.* 1.1); from living in the ceremonial booths at Sukkoth (*Sukk.* 2.8); shaking the *lulab* (tos. *Kidd.* 1.10); sounding the *shofar* (tos. *RH* 4.1); and even, at a later stage, of pronouncing the daily affirmation of faith, the *Shema* (*Ber.* 3.3).[24] Women's exemption from these time-geared precepts was the result both of their extensive periods of ritual impurity and of their designated role as closeted homemakers – though of course in making such a statement, we immediately involve ourselves in a greater degree of circularity. Anyway, unclean and in a state of domestic seclusion, they thus became increasingly less involved in matters of public religion, and the situation quickly developed wherein their non-participation was viewed in terms of actual exclusion rather than mere exemption.[25] Now, therefore, and unlike the earlier period, only men were the full participants in and officiants of the nation's religious life. In other words, they comprised the religious community; they were the sons of the new covenant as developed in the exile and beyond.

The mark of this new covenant was (and still is) circumcision. Circumcision as a rite had been performed in Israel for many centuries, but it was only with the exile that it assumed the character of a covenantal sign between God and his chosen people. Prior to that it had been viewed in terms of an individual's placatory act of redemption to the deity (or deities) and later as a rite of initiation into the tribe, so marking the male's passage firstly to ordinary, profane existence and secondly to full, public and potentially active membership of society.[26] Already at this stage of the rite's evolution, the absence of a similar rite or substitute ceremony for the girl was a loaded omission.[27] But it was the final stage in the history of circumcision which was to have the most far-reaching implications for the woman and her role in the society and religion of her people. In the exile it was decreed that circumcision was to be *the* official rite of initiation into Judaism and all that that now meant. It is in Genesis 17.10ff – the verses which are usually taken as belonging to the Priestly strand of the Bible – that we first find mention of the covenantal aspects of circumcision:

> And God said unto Abraham . . . This is My Covenant, which ye shall keep between Me and you and thy seed after thee: every male among you shall be circumcised. And ye shall be circumcised in the flesh of your foreskin; and it shall be a token of a covenant betwixt Me and you. And he that is eight days old[28] shall be circumcised among you, every male throughout your generations, he that is born in thy house, or bought with the money of any foreigner, that is not of thy seed . . . And the uncircumcised male who is not circumcised in the flesh of his

foreskin, that soul shall be cut off from his people; he hath broken my covenant.

Henceforth, and unlike the earlier period, this was to be the dominant aspect of the rite. Now it was not simply the male, but the circumcised male who was to be the full participant in his nation's covenantal law and cultic activities. So, for example, with regard to observance of the Passover, the pre-exilic ruling was for 'thee and thy son', with no further qualification, to keep the feast, whereas in the exilic and post-exilic legislation the ordinance was modified to count only those who had been circumcised.[29] Similarly, only circumcised men were under an obligation to fulfil the whole law[30] (and here I would remind you that the essence of Judaism was now legalism and observance of the commandments). In other words, they formed the public religious community, and so the words 'covenant' and 'circumcision' are often used interchangeably in the post-exilic writings.[31]

Another aspect of this later circumcision of particular pertinence to the present discussion is that removal of the foreskin did not on its own render the rite effective. In line with the general emphasis on blood in the exilic Priestly tradition, tremendous importance was attached to the actual blood of the circumcision, and unless several drops of blood were seen to issue from the wound, the operation was deemed invalid and valueless. Later it was even specified that should there be for any reason no foreskin to sever, blood must still be made to flow for a rite to be effected and for the individual to enter the covenant.[32] Whilst blood would appear to have been associated with circumcision from the earliest times (witness the account of Zipporah in *Exodus* 4.24–6),[33] this character of the rite, as I hope shortly to show, assumed new dimensions and significances with the experience of the exile and the developments which I have just outlined.

As a clue to that significance we might first recall the way in which the laws regarding menstruation and childbirth and this new circumcision appeared at the same time in the history of the Jewish people, and remember what was earlier said about the nature – culture dichotomy and the need of culture to control or impose itself upon what it deems to be nature. Both of these points need to be placed in context of the general significance which blood, of certain types, had within Hebrew thought and society. As has been shown above, blood was perceived to be the life-giving force of the universe – an obvious conclusion on empirical grounds, but one which was elevated from the pragmatic to the sacred in Hebrew thought by the belief that in humans it was also the seat of the soul, hence the choice of terminology noted at the outset of this essay for murder and death in the Old Testament. The blood of animals was also sacred, or seen as belonging particularly to the deity, and so its shedding played a central role in Jewish cult. As we have seen, differences were made regarding the value of male sacrifices as opposed to female ones, the latter only being offered on less important or *non-community* based occasions. This cultic shedding of blood was controlled by men, and consecration to the priesthood was effected by daubing men with the blood of slaughtered animals.

Taking these several points in combination we come to the particular significance of the shedding of blood in the ritual of circumcision. The belief was that to ritually and voluntarily – and I stress the word 'voluntarily' – shed one's own blood was to recommend oneself to and establish a link with the Creator of the Universe, and this is precisely what happened with circumcision.[34] In other words, by the culture-controlled shedding of blood at circumcision, the individual entered the covenant and joined with his fellow 'circumcisees', who together formed a community or brotherhood of blood, bound to each other and God by special duties and mutual obligations. Most importantly, this brotherhood was seen as extending laterally across a generation, vertically to fathers, grandfathers, sons and grandsons, and ultimately to God – a point to which I shall return.[35] The new significance of the covenantal blood of circumcision was clearly demonstrated by the later midrashic (rabbinic) paraphrase of the biblical 'life is in the blood' to 'life is in the blood of circumcision'.[36]

At precisely the same time as circumcision and the blood of circumcision was receiving this new casting and additional dimension, legislation about female blood – i.e. the blood of menstruation and childbirth – appeared for the first time on the scene. But the attention paid to it was of a completely different nature to that accorded to male blood. As we have seen, *it* was declared unclean and ritually polluting, and equated metaphorically with the defilement imparted by carrying an idol.[37] Unlike the cultic *inclusion* of men through the blood of circumcision, the blood of the female cycle resulted in cultic *exclusion* for women. So, according to the laws of Leviticus, women were forbidden to enter the Temple or touch any hallowed thing during their times of menstrual uncleanness,[38] whilst with regard to childbirth they were similarly removed from cultic activity, this time for forty days following delivery of a boy and significantly eighty days after that of a girl.[39] And here I would like to quote the Levitical ruling on childbirth for it highlights what I hope is now becoming clear, i.e. the perceived gender differentials in blood and the connection between male circumcision and the female blood cycle:

> If a woman be delivered and bear a man-child, then she shall be unclean for seven days; as in the days of the impurity of her sickness shall she be unclean. And in the eighth day the flesh of his foreskin shall be circumcised. And she shall continue in the blood of purification three and thirty days; she shall touch no hallowed thing, nor come into the sanctuary, until the days of her purification be fulfilled. But if she bear a maid-child, then she shall be unclean two weeks, as in her impurity; and she shall continue in the blood of purification threescore and six days. And when the days of her purification are fulfilled, for a son or for a daughter, she shall bring a lamb of the first year for a burnt offering, and a young pigeon or a turtledove, for a sin offering, unto the door of the tent of meeting, unto the priest. And he shall offer it before the Lord, and make atonement for her; and she shall be cleansed from the fountain of her blood . . . the priest shall make atonement for her, and she shall become clean. (Lev. 12.2ff)

The significant points to note from this passage are firstly the way in which the blood of delivery is unclean; secondly the way in which in the case of a boy's birth circumcision intrudes in the text and interrupts both the period of the mother's pollution and the account of that pollution; and thirdly, the way in which the woman is finally cleansed of her impurity through the blood of sacrifice as administered by a circumcised male.

It is apparent, therefore, that differentiation was made between male and female blood, and that circumcision, in its new casting, had some role to play in that context. To deal with the blood differential first: according to the later thinking of the *tannaim* (rabbis of the first centuries AD), the reason for the Levitical laws of menstruation and childbirth was as punishment for the sin of Eve who brought about the death of Adam. In other words, and I quote, '. . . because she shed his blood, she was punished through her blood' (*Gen. Rabbah* 17.13). As the quotation shows, the two types of blood were perceived as two sides of the same coin: on the one side positive male blood and on the other negative female blood.[40] However, whilst the image of the 'head and tail' coin is pertinent to our understanding of the rituals, the rabbis' words provide us with little more than an appreciation of how Jewish society (or a part thereof) at the time perceived and explained the religious state of affairs. In other words, they merely represent a constructed rationale of an existing custom. To reach a fuller understanding of the blood differential – its origin, purpose and effect – it is necessary to dig a little deeper and attempt to trace the underlying reasons by means of a sociological/anthropological analysis – and this is what I have been attempting to do in the course of this essay. I would now like to reiterate and elaborate the several points which I have raised so far, and then finally bring my argument round to demonstrating the link which exists between circumcision and menstrual/childbirth taboos.

The first point is that it is generally recognized that ritual tends to increase, intensify and shift in focus at times of social crisis. In particular – and on this see the work of Mary Douglas – when the body politic is threatened, it is common to see increased attention paid to the purity, integrity and unity of the physical body.[41] This, as we have seen, is precisely what happened with the exile and in the Levitical legislation regarding ritual pollution.

Secondly, ritual, in addition to mirroring the anxieties of society, also expresses the ordering of society in all its aspects and complexity, and to use the words of Ortner, may be viewed as marking the universal human endeavour to transcend and control the world of nature (amongst other things). Indeed, to continue with Ortner's words, 'the distinctiveness of culture rests precisely on the fact that it can under most circumstances transcend natural conditions and turn them to its purpose. Thus culture at some level of awareness asserts itself to be not only distinct from but superior to nature, and that sense of distinctiveness and superiority rests precisely on the ability to transform – to "socialize" and "culturalize" – nature',[42] i.e. to be active and in control.

Within this scheme of thought, anything which cannot be controlled is labelled dangerous and marginal, particularly when society is working to preserve its unity and to develop more sophisticated systems of self-definition, as was the case for the Jewish community in Palestine following the exile. The blood of childbirth and menstruation, which follows a passive and unstoppable cycle, can be construed (by the powers that be) to fall within this category, and so it is required that cultural regulation step in with restrictive legislation. That cultural regulation, as we have seen, is controlled by men, for (and this brings me to the third point), within this scheme of thought, woman herself is placed more fully within the realm of nature than man in consequence of the fact that more of her time and her body are seen to be taken up with the natural processes surrounding reproduction of the species.[43] Man, on the other hand, who within this particular characterization of the nature–culture dichotomy is deemed to lack such natural and visible creative functions, is obliged, or at least has the opportunity, (to use the words of Ortner) to assert his creativity externally through the medium of technology, ritual and symbol.[44] As active manipulator of his existence, he falls within the realm of culture, and so, just as culture is deemed superior to nature, so man and his activities are considered superior to woman and her world.[45]

And this brings me to my fourth point, and that is the notion of domestic – public opposition. Following the exile, it should be recalled that women, for a complex of pragmatic reasons, were confined almost exclusively to the domestic realm. This relegation – for as such it was undoubtedly construed[46] – to the domestic realm, whilst on the one hand promoting a higher status than before for women in terms of motherhood (a status generated for society's structural purposes and needs[47]), also resulted in an overall decrease in women's status generally, for, to use the well known Levi-Straussian model, the domestic unit – i.e. the 'biological' family concerned with reproducing and socializing new members of society[48] – was seen as separate from the public entity – i.e. the superimposed network of alliances and relationships which comprised society proper, as it were. And this separation – or indeed opposition – according to Levi-Strauss, had the significance of the opposition between nature and culture.[49] Women's world could therefore be seen as inferior to the higher cultural activities of men in the public domain[50] – a fact recognized by the first century AD Jewish philosopher Philo who in his writings made much play of this gender-differentiated opposition between the public and private domains.[51] The same writer, as we have seen (pp. 25–6 above), also elaborated at length on the idea of superior male rationality and causality versus inferior female irrationality and passivity. And this brings me finally to the link between circumcision and menstrual taboo.

Whilst women's role as mothers was of paramount importance to society – particularly after the exile when maternity, for various pragmatic reasons, became the means of transmitting and establishing in biological terms, as it were, religious and ethnic identity[52] – it would seem logical, given our culture – nature opposition and the fact that culture seeks to control and impose upon whatever has been construed as natural, that something had to be done in cultural terms about the natural function of childbirth. And this, I think, is where circumcision comes in. It served as a rite of cultural rebirth by which the male individual was accorded entry into the society and religion of his people. In other words, whilst women, as it were, merely conducted the animal-like repetitive tasks of carrying on the reproduction of the human race, men, by one supreme symbolic act, imposed themselves upon nature and enacted a cultural rebirth. The blood of circumcision served as a symbolic surrogate for the blood of childbirth, and because it was shed voluntarily and in a controlled manner, it transcended the bounds of nature and the passive blood flow of the mother at delivery and during the preparatory cycle for pregnancy, menstruation.[53] The blood of circumcision, just like the blood of animal sacrifice, could also be viewed as cleansing the boy of his mother's blood and acting as a rite of separation, differentiating him from the female, and allying him with the male community.[54] In a sense, therefore, circumcision actually creates a more powerful gender distinction rather than just deriving from such a distinction – but here again one gets wrapped in inevitable strands of circularity. For all of these reasons, and unlike the earlier biblical period, only men were allowed to perform the operation (see *Kidd.* 1.7, 29ab; *Pes.* 3.7). At a later time it was even decreed that should there be no male (in particular a father) available to sever the foreskin and make the blood flow, then the child should wait until he had grown up and then perform the operation himself. Under no circumstances was the mother to enact this cultural role.[55] All of this was so very different from the earlier period of Hebrew history when the first recorded occasion of a circumcision had as its central active character the woman Zipporah, and it puts in context the biblical passage, written at the time of the exile, with which this essay opened: Jerusalem, allegorized as a female in needy relation to her Lord and depicted as cleansed of her blood by the intervention of a male deity.

In the context of post-exilic Judaism, therefore, natural birth gave rise to an intergenerational line of blood; cultural rebirth created a network of brotherhood of blood which transcended generations and was superior to biological and socio-biological kinship ties. These were the two sides of the same coin which I referred to at the beginning of this essay, the nature – culture opposition and the particular characterizations and choice of emphases here explored being one explanation for the apparent gender differentials in blood within Jewish ritual practice, and one link at least between the rite of circumcision and menstrual taboo. The fact that both rituals continued to be practised even after the 70 AD fall of the Temple in Jerusalem when other cult-associated rituals fell into disuse and when the overt reason, at least, for the laws of female purity no longer pertained, demonstrates their central significance to the Jewish system of gender creation and differentiation – and the real hidden agenda behind their initial promulgation in the sixth century BC.

The menstrual taboo, originally presented and applied with explicit reference to maintaining the purity of the Temple and its cultic participants, was in the first century AD recast in terms of family law and the purity of marriage within the domestic unit. Its rationale shifted but its purpose in one respect at least remained, and orthodox women to this day follow through the ritual of purification at the *mikva* every month and abstain from physical contact with their husbands during their times of bleeding and for seven days thereafter (= two weeks every month).[56] In non-orthodox circles also the blood taboo, in culturally received if not strictly religious terms, is strong and is observed to varying degrees in context of inter-personal relations.

With regard to circumcision, this too remains a central ritual. Unlike the laws of menstruation and childbirth, it had never been as intimately linked to cultic activity/purity and so no recasting was required following the events of 70 AD. It remained the sign of the covenant and as such was observed in fulfilment of divine commandment, and this remains the case today among the religious. In non-religious circles, however, it is also widely practised and families who often observe little else of the religion frequently have their male children circumcised, again as part of a cultural inheritance and as a means (usually undefined and inarticulated) of self- and collective identification. Similarly, in the various schools of reform Judaism circumcision still occupies a central place, despite the objections raised by the nineteenth-century originators of the movement to the rite's continuation on the grounds (amongst others) that there was no rite of initiation for daughters into the religion so the male ritual ought to be abandoned.[57] The continued practice underlies Spinoza's belief that observance of this rite was alone sufficient to ensure the survival of the Jewish people (*Tractatus Theologico-Politicus* 3:53),[58] and demonstrates the strength of the ritual's cultural entrenchment. Whilst some shifts in meaning have occurred, therefore, the survival of the rituals of both circumcision and menstruation demonstrates their profound significance to the Jewish socio-religious and cultural system of belief and definition, and their on-going role in the business of gender and the creation of non-ambiguous male–female categories. They continue to have an impact on women's involvement in public religion and on social attitude towards 'the female'.

Finally, and to return to the first century AD, although Christianity inherited much from its Judaic roots, it did not embrace the need for circumcision. Formal, and informal, taboos around menstruation to some extent continued, but the ritual of male circumcision was abandoned – a fascinating development given the significance and purpose of the ritual and one that looks, at first glance, like a clean break with the past to facilitate the future and the expansion of Christianity (see, for example, Acts 10–11, 15; Romans 4; Gal. 3, 5). Whatever the pragmatics of the decision, however, a closer look at the New Testament and the justification which the early Christians chose to give for abandoning circumcision reveals much about the ritual and ironically brings us back full circle to the notion of gendered blood and the whole culture–nature : male–female scenario. For the ultimate cultic sacrifice and voluntary shedding of blood was seen to have been achieved in the figure of the male, circumcised, saviour Christ. He was the new and eternal Paschal lamb, he was the new Temple and law; through his blood the new covenant was established and by his blood sins were forgiven (see Heb. *passim*; 1 Cor. 5.7; Rev. 1.5, 5.6f; 14; Eph. 2; 1 John 1.7, etc.). Thinking they were breaking with the past, the early Christians re-enacted it.

Depicted as a High Priest and son of the 'King of Kings . . . clad in a robe sprinkled with blood', Christ

> . . . entered once for all into the Holy Place, taking not the blood of goats and calves but his own blood, thus securing an eternal redemption . . . He is the mediator of a new covenant . . . He has appeared once for all at the end of the age to put away sin by the sacrifice of himself . . . by the blood of the eternal covenant. (Heb. 9.12ff, 15, 26, 13.20; cf. Rev. 19.13, 16)

The old blood covenant had gone. A new one rose to replace it.

NOTES

1 For a history of source criticism and other methodological approaches to the OT, in particular the Pentateuch, see Douglas A. Knight and Gene M. Tucker (eds), *The Hebrew Bible and its Modern Interpreters*, Philadelphia and Chico, Fortress, 1985, especially ch. 8; for details regarding recent debates over the dating of the Priestly literature (which vary from pre-Deuteronomic to Persian, but with the majority of scholars still looking to the exilic and post-exilic age) and discussion as to whether P is a source or redaction, see especially pp. 285–6.
2 I say 'male' circumcision because this was the only form of circumcision practised among the Hebrews/Jews: the ancient geographer Strabo is certainly incorrect in his view that both male and female children were circumcised (*Geographica*, *XVI*, 2:37, 4:9; *XVII*, 2:5). Even if he were correct it is clear from surveys of other cultures that female circumcision has a very different function from the male rite with which we are here concerned. On this point, see Nawal El Saadawi, *The Hidden Face of Eve: Women in the Arab World*, London, Zed Press, 1980.
3 Philo, *De Specialibus Legibus*, I:226ff.
4 Philo, *De Specialibus Legibus*, I:198ff.
5 See Sherry Ortner, 'Is Female to Male as Nature is to Culture?' in Michelle Zimbalist Rosaldo and Louise Lamphere (eds), *Women, Culture and Society*, Stanford, University Press, CA, 1974, pp. 67–87. Opponents of her argument who are disinclined to use any universalistic model and who argue that Ortner simply swapped one set of deterministic principles (biological) for another equally inflexible set (social constructionist) include Janet Sayers, *Biological Politics*, London, Tavistock Publications, 1982; and Carol P. MacCormack, 'Nature, Culture and Gender: A Critique' in Carol MacCormack and Marilyn Strathern (eds), *Nature, Culture and Gender* (Cambridge University Press, 1980), pp. 1–24. The model here presented and then applied is a modified version of Ortner's which attempts to avoid some of the obvious pitfalls of her early argument whilst at the same time acknowledging its debt to her work.

6 See Ortner, p. 71: '... [biological] facts and differences only take on significance of superior/inferior within the framework of culturally defined value systems'; Kirsten Hastrup, 'The Semantics of Biology: Virginity', in Shirley Ardener (ed.), *Defining Females*, London, Croom Helm [for] the Oxford University Women's Studies Committee, 1978; p. 49: '... socially significant distinctions are mapped on to basic biological differences and vice versa'; and MacCormack, p. 18: '... the link between nature and women is not a "given". Gender and its attributes are not pure biology. The meanings attributed to male and female are as arbitrary as are the meanings attributed to nature and culture.'

7 For fuller details than is possible here of this involvement and the subsequent developments presented below, see Leonie J. Archer, 'The Role of Jewish Women in the Religion, Ritual and Cult of Graeco-Roman Palestine' in Averil Cameron and Amelie Kuhrt (eds), *Images of Women in Antiquity* (London, Croom Helm, 1983), pp. 273–87. For women active in public capacities generally, see M.C. Astour, 'Tamar the Hierodule', *Journal of Biblical Literature* 85 (1966), pp. 185–96; B.A. Brooks, 'Fertility Cult Functionaries in the Old Testament', *JBL*, 60 (1941), pp. 227–53; I.J. Peritz, 'Women in the Ancient Hebrew Cult', *JBL* 17 (1898), pp. 111–47.

8 Or at least if not the direct result they received their final and decisive impulse from the experience of the exile. Religious and social ordering had been slowly changing in the immediately preceding centuries, but the exile both accelerated and fixed these developments and marked a definite turning point. On this see further below and Leonie J. Archer, 'The Virgin and the Harlot in the Writings of Formative Judaism', *History Workshop Journal* 24 (Autumn 1987), pp. 1–16.

9 In saying that these laws were in fact exilic, I again follow both the traditional dating within the documentary hypothesis framework and, more importantly, the internal dynamic or logic of the sociological argument here elucidated.

10 Note that only the élite of the nation had been taken into exile by Nebuchadnezzar, leaving behind 'vinedressers, husbandmen, and the poorest sort of the people of the land' (2 Kings 24.14, 25.12). Of these exiles only a portion then returned to the land to start the process of purification and separation. For this see the accounts of Ezra and Nehemiah.

11 See Mary Douglas, *Purity and Danger*, (London, Routledge, 1966), p. 124, for the way in which concern about orifices, fluids, etc., mirrors the anxieties of a 'hard-pressed minority'.

12 Douglas, p. 14.

13 Douglas, p. 4. Of particular importance to us here, of course, is the need to create distinct male – female categories.

14 For an analysis of the dietary laws along these lines, see Douglas, ch. 3.

15 See the constant admonitions to this effect in Ezra, Nehemiah and throughout the Priestly strands of the OT, particularly Leviticus. For the equation by the legislators of ritual cleanness with holiness, see

Jacob Neusner, *The Idea of Purity in Ancient Judaism*, with a critique and commentary by Mary Douglas (Leiden, 1983).

16 The rules specific to men concerned excretions from the sexual organs (i.e. venereal disease) and issues of semen (Lev. 15.3–18). The first necessitated counting 'seven days for his cleansing' whilst the second, obviously more common state, resulted in impurity only 'until the even', i.e. the first sunset following the emission. The rules which pertained specifically to women will be treated below.

17 Douglas argues (*Purity and Danger*, p. 101) that women are particularly affected because their bodies serve as biological models or symbols for the purity of society – and so by implication they are the special target of such legislation. The dangers of such an argument are, however, all too obvious in that it implies an inescapable destiny for women. I prefer the focus here taken which emphasizes both the socio-economic dynamic and the cultural mapping on to the biological, in particular the patriarchal cultural mapping.

18 Here again, unlike Douglas et al., I would stress that this is just one possible interpretation of the biological facts.

19 See, for example, the analysis by Douglas of various modern societies: '... those holding office in the explicit part of the structure tend to be credited with consciously controlled powers, in contrast to those whose role is less explicit and who tend to be credited with unconscious powers, menacing those in better defined positions ... [for example:] the Kachin wife. Linking two disparate power groups, her husband's and her brother's, she holds an interstructural role, and she is thought of as the unconscious, involuntary agent of witchcraft. Similarly, the father in the matrilineal Trobrianders and Ashanti, and the mother's brother in patrilineal Tikopia and Taleland, is credited with being an involuntary source of danger. These people are none of them without a proper niche in the total society. But from the perspective of one internal sub-system to which they do not belong, but in which they must operate, they are intruders ... the kind of powers attributed to them symbolize their ambiguous, inarticulate status' (*Purity and Danger*, pp. 101–2).

20 For the rise of this concept/image and its use in creating distinct gender categories and social roles, see Archer, 'The Virgin and the Harlot ...', pp. 1–16.

21 For details of this evolution, which can only be touched upon here, and the sharp impulse provided by the exile see Archer, *Her Price is Beyond Rubies: The Jewish Woman in Graeco-Roman Palestine*, Sheffield (Academic Press, 1990), ch. 1 sect. d.

22 For detailed argument regarding these developments within a clear chronological framework (seventh century BC forward), together with biblical and post-biblical references too numerous to cite here, see Archer, 'The Virgin and the Harlot ...', pp. 5–7 with notes.

23 For the way in which the law was the hallmark of Judaism – a situation very different from the earlier Hebrew religion – , see Archer, 'The Virgin and the Harlot ...', pp. 5–7, and 'The Role of Jewish Women', p. 277.

24 For further details of these and the other exemptions, with full rabbinic references and secondary source citation, see Archer, 'The Role of Jewish Women', pp. 277ff.

25 As much is implied by various writers of the period (see Archer, *Her Price is Beyond Rubies*, ch. 1 sect. d). Note also the rabbinic view that if a woman did perform a commandment from which she was 'exempt', the action was without value for she was as 'one who is not commanded and fulfils' (*Sot.* 21a).

26 For this early history plus details of the rite's subsequent development, see Archer, *Her Price is Beyond Rubies*, ch. 1 sect. b.

27 Possible alternative rituals or *rites de passage* suggested in my book might have included, for example, the ceremonial cutting off of the girl's first hair, given that hair in the Hebrew belief system had ritual and mystical significance (*Her Price is Beyond Rubies*, ch. 1 sect. b).

28 For the significance of the operation being performed on the eighth day of the child's life rather than at any other time, see *Her Price is Beyond Rubies*, ch. 1 sect. b.

29 Contrast Exod. 12.24 (= J, early strand) with Exod. 12.44 (P). Cf. Exod. 23.17, 34.23; Deut. 16.17, all of which are pre-exilic. Note that if women did attend the Passover ceremonial in Jerusalem, they attended by virtue of some attachment to a man (husband, father, brother). See Judah Ben-Siyyon Segal, *The Hebrew Passover from the Earliest Times to AD 70*, London, 1963, p. 35.

30 See, for example, the later statement of Gal. 5.3. Note also the way in which God-fearers who attached themselves to the Jewish community but who were not under an obligation to fulfil the whole law were characterized by various ancient writers as 'the uncircumcised' (see Emil Schurer in *The History of the Jewish People in the Age of Jesus Christ*, G. Vermes, F. Millar, M. Goodman (eds), Edinburgh, T. & T. Clark, *III*.2, pp. 165ff).

31 It should be said that the uncircumcised Jew remained a Jew by birth (see *Hull.* 4b; *Ab.Zarah* 27a, and n. 52 below), but he was denied access to the higher life, as it were, of his people (i.e. like a woman). The penalty for non-observance of the rite was *karet* (Gen. 17.14) which was interpreted by the rabbis to mean premature death at the hands of heaven.

32 *Shabb.* 135–7; *Yeb.* 71a; *Gen.Rabbah* 46.12, 'The sages have taught thus: in the case of an infant born without a foreskin it is necessary *to cause a few drops of the blood of the covenant to flow from him on account of the covenant of Abraham.*' All the texts refer to 'the blood of the covenant'. On this and the sacrificial character of the rite, see Geza Vermes, *Scripture and Tradition in Judaism*, (Leiden, 1961), pp. 190–191.

33 Exod. 4.24–6, 'And it came to pass on the way at the lodging place that the Lord met him [Moses] and sought to kill him. Then Zipporah [Moses' wife] took a flint and cut off the foreskin of her son and cast it at his [Moses'/angel's?] feet, and she said "Surely a bridegroom of blood art thou to me ... A bridegroom of blood in regard to

circumcision.' Later sources (Targum, Septuagint) also emphasize the all-important role which the blood of circumcision had in Moses' redemption. On the complexities of this passage and its treatment by post-biblical writers, see Vermes, *Scripture and Tradition*, pp. 180ff, and H. Kosmala, 'The Bloody Husband', *Vetus Testamentum* 12 (1962).

34 Strictly speaking of course the eight-day-old child could not 'voluntarily' shed his own blood, but the assumption was that if he were able to determine his own fate, he would so choose. In any case, whether it was the child's will or not, the event still marked the operation of culture over nature, albeit in this instance through the agency of others.

35 So, for example, see Mal. 2.10 ('Have we not all one father? Hath not one God created us? Why do we deal treacherously every man against his brother, profaning the covenant of our fathers?'); Amos 1.9 (the 'brotherly covenant', *berith achim*); Ezekiel 18.4 ('Behold all souls are mine; as the soul of the father is mine, so also the soul of the son is mine.').

36 *Lev. Rabbah*, Lev. 17.11. Note also the way in which both midrashic (rabbinic commentary) and targumic (interpretative Aramaic translation of the Bible) exegesis saw Israel as having been saved through the blood of Passover *and* the blood of circumcision. See Vermes, *Scripture and Tradition*, pp. 190–191. We might also note that in the eyes of the midrashic commentators, not only were the Hebrews in Egypt saved by the smearing of the blood of male animals on the doorposts but, in opposition, God had 'punished the Egyptians with blood' because they had not allowed the daughters of Israel to ritually immerse themselves following menstruation (*Ex. Rabbah* 9.10).

37 So, for example, the statement of R. Akiba in *Shabb.* 9.1. For biblical instances of the uncleanness of the menstruant being used as a noun and metaphor for the height of defilement, see Ezek. 7.19–20; Lam. 1.17; Ezra 9.11; 2 Chron. 29.5 (note that all of these works are to be dated to the exile and beyond).

38 Lev. 15.19–32. Biblical law declared the woman unclean just for the days of bleeding, up until the close of a seven-day period (if bleeding continued thereafter she entered a different category of uncleanness); rabbinic law, however, around the turn of the eras and the first centuries of the Christian period extended the time of uncleanness to count from the day the woman expected her menses through to the close of seven clear days (i.e., days without bleeding), and totalled the whole period of impurity as a minimum of twelve days, the ruling that applies today. The emphasis of the biblical law (our concern here) was with admission to the cult, that of the rabbis with sexual activity between husband and wife, a shift that will be touched on further below. For details of the consequences of impurity, its transmission to others, etc., see *Encyclopaedia Judaica* vol. 12, cols. 1141–7, vol. 13 cols. 1405–12.

39 For an analysis of the social significance of this differentiation, see Archer, *Her Price is Beyond Rubies*, ch. 1 sect. b.

40 We might note that despite the wording of this particular quotation, used by the rabbis for a specific purpose, Eve is *not* in the main cited as the culprit for the Fall, rather the attention of the texts lies with Adam. The shift in focus to Eve only came about with Christianity and the work of the Church Fathers. On this see Archer, 'The Virgin and the Harlot . . .', p. 2 and n. 5.
41 Douglas, *Purity and Danger*, especially chs 7 and 9.
42 Ortner, pp. 72–3.
43 See Simone de Beauvoir, *The Second Sex*, (London, Cape, 1968), pp. 24ff, regarding the non-function to the individual of breasts, ovarian secretions, menstrual cycle, etc., and her conclusion (p. 239) that the female '. . . is more enslaved to the species than the male, her animality is more manifest'. Note the way in which I, along with Ortner (pp. 73ff), would stress that woman within this scheme of thought is seen as *closer* to nature and not relegated totally to that realm. As Levi-Strauss writes, no matter how devalued woman and her designated role may be, or how denied her ability to transcend and socialize, '. . . even in a man's world she is still a person, and since insofar as she is defined as a sign she must [still] be recognized as a generator of signs' (in *Elementary Structures of Kinship*, Boston, Beacon Press, 1969, p. 496). The tensions inherent to this conceptual system and the woman's intermediary and interstructural role (noted already) are obvious.
44 Ortner, p. 75.
45 Note in this context de Beauvoir's comments regarding the way in which greater prestige is often accorded to the male destruction of life (e.g. warfare, hunting, etc.) than to the female creation of life (*The Second Sex*, pp. 58–9), and Ortner's comments thereto (p. 75). This is a particularly salient point remembering what has here been said regarding cultic sacrifice and its practitioners. In some feminist circles there have been moves towards reversing this situation by the introduction of formalized and ritualized celebrations of female creativity and the menstrual cycle. See Rosemary Radford Ruether in this volume.
46 See, for example, Josephus, *Con. Ap.* 2.201, 'The woman, says the Law, is in all things inferior to the man'; Philo, *Spec. Leg.* 3:169f (quoted n. 51 below). For an argument against the spurious but oft-heard 'different but equal' thesis see Leonie J. Archer, 'Women in Formative Judaism' (unpublished paper, Oxford 1986).
47 See the marked frequency with which the community was reminded in the exilic and post-exilic writings of the command to 'Honour thy father and thy mother', and Archer, *Her Price is Beyond Rubies*, ch. 1 sect. d and ch. 2 sect. a for an analysis of both the commandment's social dynamic and the qualified nature in fact of the respect to be accorded the woman. See also n. 50 below.
48 Levi-Strauss's labelling of the domestic unit as 'biological' is of course too simplistic and indeed predisposes his own conclusion. It is also internally contradictory to his own definition which includes the domestic unit's socializing function. To follow his labelling would be to

place women (and other members of the family) totally within the realm of nature. Bearing in mind these drawbacks, though, the model remains extremely useful and insightful.
49 Levi-Strauss, p. 479, quoted in Ortner, p. 78.
50 On this see Michelle Zimbalist Rosaldo, 'Woman, Culture, and Society: A Theoretical Overview', in Rosaldo and Lamphere, *Women, Culture and Society*, pp. 17–42; Nancy Chodorow, 'Family Structure and Feminine Personality', in ibid., pp. 43–66; Ortner, 'Is Female to Male...' The focus on women's role/status as mother also encouraged this view, for the tendency was to regard the tasks of motherhood as purely natural without recognizing that the bulk of the work involved socializing new members of the community.
51 See, for example, *Spec. Leg.* 3:169f, 'Market places and council halls and law courts and gatherings and meetings where a large number of people are assembled, and open air life with full scope for discussion and action – all these are suitable for men both in war and peace. The women are best suited to the indoor life which never strays from the house ... Organized communities are of two sorts, the greater which we call cities and the smaller which we call households. Both of these have their governors; the government of the greater is assigned to men under the name of statesmanship, that of the lesser, known as household management, to women ...'
52 Regarding the question of Jewish identity, we should note that at least by Talmudic times (fifth century AD), the (ethnic) status of the child was determined by that of his or her mother and not by the father. So *Kidd.* 68b (on the basis of the second century AD mishnah), 'Thy son by an Israelite woman is called thy son, thy son by a Gentile woman is not called thy son.' According to *Encyclopaedia Judaica* vol. 10 cols. 54–5 such halachic definition of Jewish identity had been reached by Hasmonaean times (second – first centuries BC). Although more research needs to be done regarding exactly when this understanding of ethnic transmission was introduced – especially given the current debate over 'Who is a Jew?' – it is certainly possible that it evolved around the time of the exile and the community's return to Palestine.
53 Although often coming from a completely different analytical perspective from the one here taken, it is interesting and revealing to note the way in which the ritual is popularly described in the secondary sources. For example. E.O. James in *Myth and Ritual*, S.H. Hooke, ed., London, 1933, p. 150 writes, 'In most communities where the corporate attitude of mind still predominates it is necessary for the individual at some period of his [sic] life ... to undergo a solemn initiation into the tribal society, as distinct from that of the clan or family group in which he has been born. Until this has been done the youth is excluded from the ceremonial (i.e. the social) life of the tribe. Hence the rite consists virtually in a new birth ... as a complete and active member of society.'
54 See again Lev. 12.2ff and my analysis thereof, pp. 36–7 above. See also

J.B. Segal, 'Popular Religion in ancient Israel', *Journal of Jewish Studies* 27/1 (Autumn 1976), pp. 5–6, who descriptively rather than analytically writes: 'A male infant was circumcised on the eighth day after birth because he was affected by his mother's uncleanness during the first seven days after the delivery; the eighth day was the first on which he could be approached by the male who carried out the ceremony'.

55 See *Gen. Rabbah* 46.9 (17.8), 'Only he who is himself circumcised may perform circumcision ... An uncircumcised Israelite may not circumcise', and *Song of Songs Rabbah* 4.6, 1 (on Gen. 17.13), 'God said, 'Shall an unclean person come and operate on the clean? Would that be right? No; "circumcising he shall be circumcised" ... it befits the clean to attend the clean.'

56 See the essay by Linda Sireling in this book.

57 See *Encyclopaedia Judaica* vol. 5 cols. 570–71 and *Jewish Encyclopaedia* vol. IV p. 96 for details of the proposed reform and the degree of agitation which it engendered.

58 Cf. *Encyclopaedia Judaica* vol. 5 col. 575, '[Circumcision] is not only a religious but also a national practice, and is observed as enthusiastically by the secularists ... as by traditional believers. Its influence on Jewish life throughout the ages has been so strong that its observance is often the sole remaining token of affinity with Judaism, even after intermarriage, when the Jewish parent insists on the circumcision of the sons.'

3 Sanjukta Gupta Gombrich

Divine Mother or Cosmic Destroyer: The paradox at the heart of the ritual life of Hindu women

The Hindu view[1] of women is deeply ambivalent. This is reflected in the religion, which in turn serves as the model for traditional Hindu society. Women in Hinduism are caught up in a paradoxical view of the female, where the divine can be feminine, yet women are profoundly mistrusted.

The Goddess, in various forms, is widely worshipped amongst Hindus. Theoretically She represents and personifies divine cosmic power and sovereignty. She is God's creative energy as well as His power to destroy and at the same time she is His saving grace. The ambivalence lies in the representation of the Goddess as either alone or as the spouse of a male God. In the idiom of mythology, when the Goddess is actively destructive She is depicted alone, whereas when She is the nurturing cosmic mother and the embodiment of God's benign grace, She is represented as the spouse of a dominant male god, Shiva or Vishnu.

The most popular form of the Goddess is Durga.[2] She is the heroic Goddess who destroys all evil powers embodied as demons and She is the Goddess of victory. In Her most terrifying dark form, known as Kali, the Goddess is seen as devouring demons and surrounded by corpses. She is the embodiment of the divine cosmic power of destruction. As God's ultimate judgement She punishes the evil forces by annihilating them. Neither of these forms of the Goddess is accompanied by a male god. When warring against the demons they are accompanied by hosts of spirits who are all female.

On the other hand Uma or Parvati, the Goddess seen as the cosmic mother, is always depicted together with Her consort the cosmic god Shiva. She is beautiful and benign and the embodiment of all the finest qualities of a loyal and loving wife. In order to emphasize the motherhood of the Goddess She is sometimes accompanied by Ganesha or Skanda, her sons. As Lakshmi or

Sanjukta Gupta Gombrich

Kamala, She represents beauty, prosperity, auspiciousness and benevolence, qualities most valued in a wife. Lakshmi is usually depicted as the consort of the god Vishnu.

There are countless forms of the Goddess. She is the active power of God and She represents God's indomitable will. She carries out God's cosmic functions of creation and sustenance. Hindus believe in an endless cycle of creation and destruction. At the end of each cycle God destroys his creation which then lies dormant in Him to be recreated. The Goddess is also the instrument of such cosmic destruction. As the stern controller of cosmic justice, punishing the breakers of God's cosmic rules and order and as the frenzied cataclysmic destroyer, the Goddess functions alone.

But in her benign form the Goddess is the cosmic mother who nurtures all living creatures. For the devotees She is indulgence incarnate and She represents the divine grace that delivers creatures from worldly distress and bondage. In these latter roles She is almost always accompanied by Her divine spouse, the male God, emphasizing the fact that only in a happy marriage can the terrible and destructive aspect of the Goddess be controlled. In this essay I shall attempt to show how this need to control the female permeates the ritual life of the Hindu woman.

Hindu society is predominantly a patrifocal society, and it is usually the men who make up the socially dominant group. In this tradition the centre of authority in a family lies with the males rather than the females, although in the predominantly agricultural society in which Hinduism persisted and developed in India, women's importance in the family economy has always been considerable. In particular, their child-bearing capacity is emphatically acknowledged as the greatest contribution to familial and social welfare. The beneficial effect of a caring and nurturing mother is often stressed, assuring a high position for her in the family. The position of a wife is, on the other hand, controversial and full of conflict and trauma. Further, an unmarried woman is a social anomaly.

Hindu society is structured on the basis of its caste system. Each caste is made of a group of family lineages who are endogamous within the caste but must marry outside the paternal lineage. One

Through the Devil's Gateway

becomes a member of a caste by being born into one of its lineages which are always transmitted from male to male. A woman is born into one lineage but is transferred to her husband's lineage as soon as she is married. The wife is the means through which a man transmits his lineage to his son; she is often compared to a field in which her husband sows his seed for the continuation of his lineage.

Child-bearing is thus the primary social duty of a woman, and marriage with its corollary, the puberty rite, is the most important life-cycle ceremony in a woman's life. The little Hindu girl is brought up carefully to prepare for her role as a wife and mother in an alien family. Her loving parental home, she knows, is only a temporary shelter.

As a woman's sexuality must be controlled by the male authority who should then utilize it solely for his own benefit, in their natal home women are not sexually active. As soon as a girl reaches puberty, which is celebrated as a life cycle rite, she must be married off outside the family and its clan group. She should not and cannot be sexually active in her natal family and hence is regarded while she is there as both benign and pure.

Thus woman's sexuality is held to be her most important asset. This is celebrated in all the puberty rites observed by the Hindu girl. After the first three days she takes a purificatory bath, and then is given a complete mini-bridal trousseau by her father or, in his absence, her brother. She is given festive food and small presents by her relatives.[3] All individual rites underscore her imminent status as a wife and as a mother. She becomes aware of the importance of her body. She also begins to understand the power of her sexuality, which when purged of its impurity and wantonness can greatly enhance the life and luck of her husband. For a Hindu woman nothing is more important than possessing a husband and nothing is luckier than to have a loving and caring husband. All the marriage rites emphasize that while her fertility is her main asset, she must be faithful to her husband so that the legitimacy of her children should be beyond doubt.

The young bride in her husband's family does not automatically receive love and a secure position. She is regarded as an outsider and a probable nuisance to the solidarity of a joint family. As soon as she is married and enters her husband's family and clan group she is considered a potential source of danger, because her sexuality remains still incompletely controlled and its beneficiality as yet not proven through child-bearing.

But the situation of the young bride improves as soon as she conceives. In a Hindu family the occasion is a festive one. The expectant mother is treated with care and indulgence. Every member of the family looks after her safety as she carries the much welcome unborn child. Throughout the period of pregnancy many ritual festivities are held to ensure the pregnant mother's mental and physical well-being. In one such festival, her husband shows his love for her by presenting her with a new dress and himself attending to her hairdo and make up. This is in sharp contrast to the normal behaviour of a married couple, since modesty and decorum require them to refrain from any open show of their mutual love.

After childbirth too the mother continues to receive considerate treatment from her in-laws. A child in a Hindu family is generally an object of love and joy not only for its parents but for every member of the family. As the nurturing mother of the child a married woman is accorded esteem and care by her marital family. She is no longer regarded as an alien, and the birth of her first child brings her full social status and consolidates her position in her husband's family. A young wife with a baby is the most auspicious object. She is in great demand at Hindu social and religious functions.

A widow, on the other hand, is utterly rejected being the embodiment of bad luck. Her uncontrolled sexuality is a potential source of destruction to her family. It is compounded when she is also young and childless. Female fertility is compared with that of the mother earth. When properly cultivated and controlled by men, the earth by her nature yields a bounteous harvest. But neglected and uncontrolled the same earth very soon destroys cultivated land and human habitat with impenetrable overgrowth. In other words, nature is chaotic when not controlled by men; so also are women. Manu, the famous ancient Hindu law-giver, said that in her childhood the woman must be under the control of her father; in her adult life she must be under her husband's control and in her old age her son must control her. A woman is not fit to be free.[4] Thus Hindu society bestows on its women the paradoxical nature of having power which is both beneficial and dangerous.

For it is clear that in the traditional view a sexually mature woman should be sexually active. That is what she is assumed to

Through the Devil's Gateway

want, and that is her innate nature and hence it should be so. And thus women's sexuality is a source of constant anxiety within Hinduism. Firstly, a Hindu girl must be a virgin when she gets married. This causes a great deal of anxiety for the parents of a girl child, for they start immediately after her puberty to worry about her marriage if she is not already married. In some traditional communities, even as late as the early 1930s, unmarried girls were married off within a month or so after their first menstruation; until then, they were kept hidden inside their homes.[5]

Secondly, as mentioned before, Hindu society is patrilineal and it follows a rigid system of caste distinction. The unambiguous identity of a child's father is crucial for the child's own social identity. A woman's chastity is considered as her highest virtue and all Hindu traditional literature extols the greatness of a chaste woman. Great spiritual power is envisaged in such chastity, and hence the most virtuous woman is one who commits *sati* or *suttee*, that is, voluntary suicide committed by being cremated alive with the corpse of one's husband. It is taken to be the ultimate proof of conjugal loyalty.

Hindu society, therefore, has always shown a nervousness about the sexually active woman. Confronted by the vexing problem of needing this sexuality and fertility of women for the furtherance of the family lineage and the equally important need of their chastity for the purity of that lineage the society bestowed on their husbands total authority over them and their sexuality. This control is clearly seen in the rules surrounding menstruation.

The physical expression of female sexuality is her monthly period and its triumph lies in her giving birth. But in both these situations she is marked as unclean and is segregated, as in both cases she bleeds. Blood represents death, and all the latent male fears of women's sexuality find expression in branding her as impure and avoiding her company. She is often segregated in a hut outside the house. Menstrual blood is considered both dangerous and polluting. For the first three days of her monthly period she is segregated in a solitary place and is not allowed to touch anybody or anything lest she pollutes it.

At the end of the third day, a woman performs complicated ritual purificatory acts to cleanse herself of the pollution of menstrual blood. Often, too, women undertake a special religious vow of performing a greater number of such purity rites at a particular time of the year, followed by a ritual worship of her husband. It is as if by doing so a woman offers herself, ritually cleansed, to be entirely controlled by her husband.[6]

It was an ancient custom that on the fourth day of her menstruation, when a woman had taken her ritual bath, her husband was honour-bound to have intercourse with her. Her sexuality was supposed to be greatly intensified during the first three days and on the fourth day she was supposed to be the most fertile for conception. So it was a husband's sacred duty not to refuse her on that day even if he were practising celibacy.[7] This belief in a woman's heightened sexuality during her period may also have contributed to her being considered dangerous and hence polluting to all males.

This idea took hold especially in the early medieval period when in Hindu society asceticism and renunciation became idealized. At this time, to minimize the danger of a highly sexual woman, many taboos came into existence to restrict her movement. Female menstrual blood became endowed with magical power and often it was harmful. Sometimes it could be used even against the person to whom it belonged. A myth was revived according to which menstruation was not natural, but the result of sin. The sin, curiously enough was not committed by any woman. The sin belonged to the king of heaven, Indra, who killed a brahmin. When he wanted to get rid of the consequence of the murder, women were made to share it with two other victims. Since then women got their menstrual flow as a manifestation of their sin. Thus in an extraordinary manner the physical manifestation of a woman's fertility which had always been welcome and extolled in ancient and traditional Hindu society, where even mother earth was conceived to be menstruating in the beginning of the rainy season, came to be associated with a sin.[8]

As already mentioned, after puberty a girl does not stay long in her natal home. The tradition says she must be given in marriage as soon as possible. Old law-givers said that the father of a menstruating girl should marry her off immediately. Otherwise, each month the girl menstruates the father incurs the sin of infanticide.[9] Clearly, menstrual blood had somehow been connected with the unfertilized egg and was confused with the abortion of a foetus. Similarly, after childbirth the placenta is disposed of with great ritual care, since it is considered to be the solidified form of the mother's menstrual blood during her pregnancy. The placenta is usually called the flower, the child its fruit. Thus in both menstruation and childbirth, a woman is associated with both life and death and deemed to have dangerous power over the fate of the foetus.

A Hindu girl, approaching her teens and puberty, starts feeling nervous. On the one hand, the onset of menstruation gives her immediately the status of young womanhood. The glory and gravity of a successful married life, of wifehood and motherhood – the only traditional goal of a Hindu woman – come within her reach and dazzle her.

But on the other hand, she has her misgivings too. Until the physical appearance of puberty a girl enjoys the privilege of being regarded as an image of the great Goddess. As such, little girls have a special ritual participation in Goddess-worship, are considered a source of good luck and are even occasionally worshipped by other Hindus. But the association of menstrual blood pollutes her and she loses for ever the pristine purity of a female child. Thus the event of her puberty puts an end to her pure childhood.[10]

Thus, being so paradoxically evaluated by the external structures of their culture, women themselves suffer from an ambiguity about their sexuality and menstruation. Menstruating women refer to their state during their period as being dirty. They also believe that the safety of a husband's life and his prosperity depends on their scrupulously following all pollution taboos and keeping strictly to the purity rules.

Widows, the only social position that a traditional society could envisage for a husbandless adult woman, have always been considered as inauspicious and undesirable people. Their dangerous, uncontrolled sexuality is destined to be muted by the life-long practice of inhuman austerities and self-denial. They are shunned in any auspicious rites, especially marriage. The entire family of a widow, especially if she is still young, make it their business jealously to guard her brittle good name as a chaste woman. Whereas a woman who dies before her husband is considered to have made a good death and her body is decked in a married woman's finery, one who survives her husband is somehow always blamed for his death and must never put on finery again as a penance. Often the horror and humility of her widowhood would drive a young widow to follow her husband on his burning pyre. The glory of this status was not little.[11]

As women's prestige and prosperity entirely depend on their husband's, most of their typically religious activities have been centred on their husband's welfare. These religious rites, performed only by women, are known as *vratas*. Unmarried girls observe such *vratas* mainly to obtain a prosperous and loving husband, an indulgent and caring marital family, and to die before their husbands. Married women observe *vratas* to keep their husbands safe and healthy till they themselves die, to increase their husbands' fortune and to preserve their husbands' affection. Finally, they perform rites to obtain children, preferably male, and for the safety and health of their children.

The position of a Hindu woman in her marital family becomes vastly more secure when she becomes a mother, especially of male children. Only then does she become a full member of her husband's lineage and secure her old age even in the absence of her husband. A mother supplies her baby with the purest of all food, i.e. her breast milk. For her son she is pure and nurturing, but also a source of anxiety, since he cannot control her sexuality. Thus a widowed mother of an adult son is loved and trusted, but also sometimes feared by him. The Hindu traditional family has to live with this paradox.

A son is duty bound to look after his mother. Often tension arises between the mother and the wife of a man and no matter how unjust the attitude of the mother, society expects the son to respect his mother's wishes more than those of his wife. As a result, the conjugal relationship between the couple can suffer, and this tension can even cause mental illness. But these are exceptions, and usually, through long cohabitation, women in a single family develop a certain understanding. The mother's authority may counterbalance the otherwise all-powerful male authority in a family. In Hindu families, therefore, often the women members stand by each other in times of stress and distress.

Mothers, wives, sisters and daughters – in each of these roles Hindu women function in a paradoxical way which reflects this male attitude towards their sexuality. As sisters and daughters women are treated with respect and often indulgence but also as temporary guests. A wife, although an integral member of her husband's family, is often treated badly and with suspicion, especially while she is young. A mother is, on the other hand, held in great esteem, and even in awe.

In conclusion, one may say that in the ritual life of the traditional Hindu woman one can see the ambivalence of the traditional attitude of Hindu society towards its women and their sexuality. This attitude contains a basic paradox in regarding woman as both sacred and evil. She has the potential for fulfilling all that a man hopes to attain in his life. But she can also bring about his destruction. Like the Hindu Goddess she has both divine and demoniac qualities latent in her nature.[12] Males should judiciously manipulate her throughout her life to suppress the latter and develop the former. At all events, she should not be left alone to be just herself. Her identity in the society is as the daughter of somebody, as the wife of somebody and finally as the mother of somebody. By herself she is nobody.

Women's power lies in conforming to and consolidating these statuses. The women achieve this by the performances of countless religious rituals of their own which are observed for the welfare of their male protectors in their families. These are totally women's rituals: males are not participants but beneficiaries. In these rites women strengthen their social and familial position by underscoring their closeness to the paradoxical Goddess who is universally worshipped by Hindus.

NOTES

1 It is difficult to generalize Hinduism since it is not a monolithic religion. In fact it is a conglomerate of religions. It differs from caste to caste, region to region, rural to urban and sect to sect. One can only say that in spite of the diversity there runs through the whole gamut of religious practices a basic Hindu attitude to society, human relationships and nature. I shall be trying to present this basic view.
2 See Sanjukta Gupta and Emmie te Nijenhuis, *Sacred Songs of India: Diksitar's Cycle of Hymns to the Goddess Kamala*, Part I: Musicological and Religious Analysis, Text and Translation, Forum Ethnomusicologicum 3, (Amadeus, Winterthur (Switzerland), 1987) pp. 6–25; David Kinsley, *Hindu Goddesses: Vision of the Divine Feminine in the Hindu Religious Tradition* (Berkeley, University of California Press, 1986), *passim*.

3 Lynn Bennet, *Dangerous Wives and Sacred Sisters: Social and Symbolic Roles of High Caste Women in Nepal* (New York, Columbia University Press, 1983), pp. 214–60.
4 Manu X, 36–51. Manu was the most important ancient Indian law-giver. The text of Manu's lawbook as it has come down to our time took its final shape between 200 BC and 200 AD. This text is universally respected by all Hindu authorities on religious and social law from ancient times down to the modern period. See V. Raghavan, 'The Manu Samhita', article in S.K. De, U.N. Ghoshal, A.D. Paluskar, R.C. Hazra (eds), *The Cultural Heritage of India*, Vol. II, (The Ramakrishna Mission Institute of Culture, Calcutta, 1962) pp. 335–363.
5 Although this practice was no longer followed after the first two decades of this century the custom had earlier been practised by many very orthodox Hindu communities.
6 Bennet, *Dangerous Wives*; I. Julia Leslie, *The Perfect Wife: The Orthodox Hindu Woman according to the Stridharmapaddhati of Tryambakayajvan*. Delhi, Oxford University Press, 1989.
7 Leslie, pp. 286–8.
8 Leslie, pp. 250–51.
9 See P.V. Kane, *History of Dharma Sastra (Ancient and Medieval Religious and Civil laws)*, vol. II, part 1. Government Oriental Series class B, no. 6, Bhandarkar Oriental Research Institute, Poona, (India), 1941, p. 442.
10 The rules on menstruation pollution and its purificatory rites are followed by orthodox Hindu women even today. Although there exist great regional variations, the basic rule of the three-day pollution is followed by all. Leslie, pp. 283–8.
11 Leslie, pp. 298–304.
12 Sanjukta Gupta and Teun Goudriaan, *Hindu Tantric and Sakta Literature*. Wiesbaden (W. Germany), Otto Harrassowitz, 1981, pp. 178–9. *For further reading*: Lina M. Fruzzetti, *The Gift of A Virgin: Women, Marriage and Ritual in a Bengali Society*, New Brunswick, Rutgers University Press, 1982.

4 *Sara Maitland*

Rose of Lima: Some thoughts on purity and penance

Rose of Lima was born in Peru in 1586 and died in 1617 at the age of thirty-one. She was canonised in 1671 – the first American-born saint of the Roman Catholic Calendar – and was named principal patron of South America and the Philippines.

She remains a popular saint, not just in her native Peru, but until very recently in Europe also. There are innumerable holy cards and representations of her. She is usually shown wearing a religious habit (although she was never a nun) and either surrounded by or wearing garlands of roses. She has a modest expression and a pale sweet face. Infantilized, she used to appear regularly in hagiographical volumes, especially those designed for the edification of small girls.

All this is extremely odd. It has very little to do with her life, and they would be bizarre parents or catechetists who really wanted the girls in their charge to emulate Rose of Lima in any very direct way. Although such volumes endeavour valiantly to stress her various charitable works, especially among the enslaved and oppressed Indians, and her experiences of a mystical marriage to Christ, Rose of Lima's real claim to fame and sanctity was the extraordinary life of violent and self-inflicted penance which she maintained from extremely early in her childhood until she died.

> It was no less astonishing that she should find room on her emaciated body to engrave in it, by her discipline, the wounds of the son of God ... she gave herself such blows that her blood sprinkled the walls ... and as she practised this penance daily every night she reopened her bleeding wounds by making new ones ... Her confessor having ordered her to use an ordinary discipline and leave off her iron chain, she made it knot three rows and wore it round her body ... This chain soon took the skin off and entered so deeply into her flesh that it was no longer visible ... She bound her arms from the shoulder to the elbow with thick cords ... she rubbed herself with nettles ... [in her full

length hair shirt] she appeared more glorious in the eyes of God from her having armed it underneath with a great quantity of points of needles to increase her suffering by this ingenious cruelty ... She exposed the soles of her feet at the mouth of the oven ... she drank gall and rubbed her eyes therewith ... in her ardent desire for suffering she made herself a silver circlet in which she fixed three rows of sharp points in honour of the thirty-three years that the Son of God lived upon earth ... she wore it underneath her veil to make it the more painful as these points being unequally long did not all pierce at the same time ... so that with the least agitation these iron thorns tore her flesh in ninety-nine places ... To keep herself from sleep she suspended herself ingeniously upon a large cross which hung in her room ... and should this fail she attached her hair [the one lock she had not shaved off] to the nail in the feet of her Christ so that the least relaxation would inflict terrible suffering on her ... [She constructed herself a bed so excruciatingly painful that] although she was very generous, still she never placed herself upon it without trembling and shuddering ... so violent was the emotion which the inferior [i.e. her body] manifested at the sight of the pain it was to endure ... Rose represented forcibly the necessity she felt of suffering this continual martyrdom in order to be conformable to her divine spouse.[1] Etc., etc., etc.

This sort of 'fanatical' asceticism is currently not well received in intellectual theological circles, although popular piety is slower to abandon its old allegiances. It smacks deeply, to us post-Freudians, of the neurotic. Interestingly, fashions in asceticism do come and go. Teresa of Avila and Catherine of Siena, both of whom 'indulged' in rigorous self-discipline (and indeed it was on Catherine of Siena that Rose of Lima modelled her own life style), are none the less deeply respected. In 1970 – that is, since the reforms of the Roman Catholic Church instituted by the Second Vatican Council – they have both, unlike any other women saints, been honoured by the Church with the title of Doctor. At the same time both are frequently much admired by women looking for rôle models within the Christian tradition.

In a similar way the Desert Fathers, whose ascetical practices frequently seem to pass into the range of farce, are regarded at least with affection and more often with deep admiration, partly of course because of the delightful anecdotery that has collected around them, and is known to us through the works of writers like Helen Waddell. Francis of Assisi maintains an astonishingly high position of regard in the hearts of many Christians who would comfortably condemn Rose of Lima, despite the fact that as well as chatting to wolves and birds, his own asceticism, and that laid on his followers, was ferocious and absolute.

Now it is true that all these examples of Christian virtue had other things to offer than a rigorous asceticism and a rather overt and physical way of acting this out. Rose of Lima wrote no spiritual works; influenced, in her time at least, no worldly powers; reformed no evil Church authorities; fought no public battles; and lived anyway in a Third World country thousands of miles from the centre of things. Her life really was that of one of the *anawim*, the 'little ones' of God – and the distaste that many of us feel for her is rather like a similar distaste for Thérèse of Lisieux. Magnificence is admirable if not always comprehensible, humility is very unattractive to the modern Western mind.

The usual ways of dealing with such individuals is to ignore them, or to 'diagnose' them psychoanalytically, or to use them as 'proof' of the misogyny of the Church authorities.[2] All three of these approaches, and especially the second and third, do have their validity. Nothing of what I am going to attempt to say should in any way be read as denying the value of psychoanalysis nor as implying that the Church has not been, and continues to be, deeply misogynistic in ways that are damaging both to women and to the Church itself. Only two years ago I myself wrote an essay[3] which uses all three of these mechanisms directly about Rose of Lima: it diagnoses her 'problem' as a sado-masochistic relationship to God, it relates this causally to a religious culture which is viciously sexist and heterosexist, and it suggests that we deal with all this by growing up into spiritual maturity and putting such alarming eccentricities behind us.

The limits of this approach are extremely simple: Rose of Lima did not have a problem. I may have a problem, but that is a very different matter. It is important I think to distinguish these two quite carefully. The lives of the saints are of course available for me, or anyone else, to use in our own journeyings. There is plenty of psychoanalytical data to suggest that modern women do have a complicated relationship with sexuality involving guilt and pain of complex kinds; inasmuch as these relationships constitute barriers in the growth of a person she should seek such healing as she may be able to find. Some of that healing lies in understanding the history of both her own (Western, Christian, dualist) culture and of the construction of gender. Some of that healing lies in setting free the imagination, in using icons and images wherever they may be found, in exploring the tenuous patterns of meaning laid down in lives which no longer have a social context fully comprehensible to us. But we must not confuse any of that with a static universalist understanding of the personality, nor – out of respect for the women of our past as well as out of respect for the truth – simply write over their self-identity.

Rose of Lima did not have a problem. Quite simply, there is no evidence that this young woman had a problem as we would define it. She was not miserable; she certainly was not coerced into her life style (quite the contrary, her family made considerable effort to dissuade her, and even the Church authorities of her time were not encouraging); she was not psychopathic, in the sense that she did not inflict sufferings on other people; she was the recipient of quite remarkable consolations,[4] including that highest of all delights, the conviction of the 'mystical marriage', in which Christ takes the soul directly as his spouse, and a loving one at that.

> Jesus Christ several times appeared to her with a sweet and gracious countenance, saying to her to rouse her courage, "remember my love, that the bed of the cross on which I died for love of you was harder, narrower and more painful than that on which you are now lying".[5]

Moreover she had the real comfort of knowing that her community appreciated what she was doing; more, her life excited such admiration that after her death the interment had to be delayed for some days for fear of riots. An archbishop presided at her requiem and her bier was carried through the city by leading members of the civil authorities.

Even if we now find it difficult to accept that these were real or substantial recompenses for the life she had chosen to live we cannot reasonably question that *she* did.

Moreover if we wish to interpret 'consolations' in a rather more modern way we cannot but admire the efficiency with which she took control of her own life. The immediate and natural recourse of a woman set on a highly militant search after holiness, an escape from marriage and its social duties and a private life, would have been to enter a convent. In adolescence Rose of Lima seriously considered this option, but in fact was led by her own inner genius to reject it in favour of a hut in her own garden. It is true that by this choice she sacrificed a community life, which has for many women proved nourishing, but she also gained in personal freedom. All the evidence suggests that she had her confessor wrapped around her little finger: while claiming the complete obedience appropriate to her spiritual supervisor she in fact got round every attempt he ever made to make her moderate her life style; she persuaded him to confer his blessing and approval on her choices. By eliminating the formal codes of obedience which in the conventual life she would have owed to her mother superior *and* to the canons of her order *and* to episcopal authority, she was able to claim a more radical obedience, an obedience to God alone. By constructing her life the way she did, she evaded many of the usual controls and sanctions that governed the lives of women, her obedience was given directly to God, and her claim was that only she could interpret that obedience. In short she obtained a remarkable degree of autonomy. So much so that at one point she was actually investigated by the Inquisition – in its mildest form – who were however unable to discipline or control her life. In their report they noted that, despite her lack of education, they were unable to find any of her practices heretical and

> They also remarked with astonishment a sort of combat between God and her without being able to determine whether God was more occupied in seeking in the secrets of his wisdom the means of exercising her by suffering than she was disposed to suffer for his love; for she showed an incredible avidity for crosses and an invincible patience over her trials and over every affliction which Almighty God sent to exercise her love and fidelity.[6]

In summary, she had not only slipped away from their definitions of appropriate female behaviour, she also forced them to acknowledge a strange and unexpected relationship of equality between her and her God.

Finally Rose of Lima also had the great consolation of believing that she was doing a socially useful job – and there were not many of these available for women in the early seventeenth century. Even the somewhat pietistic Alban Butler in his *Lives of the Saints* acknowledges this:

> We admire a St Bennet on briers, a St Bernard freezing in the ice, and a St Francis in the snow, these saints were cruel to themselves not to be overcome by the devil; but Rose punishes herself to preserve others.[7]

Once again the theology on which her understanding of her own life was clearly based is one that is not deeply sympathetic to us now; nonetheless it was a deeply social, corporate and incarnational way of seeing the world. To make oneself a 'victim of God's justice', to perform penances greater than one's own sins had 'earned', was to set that additional penance 'free' for someone else to 'use' for their salvation. Rose of Lima's own understanding of this has clear biographical origins which are worth noting.

Her family, although Spanish in origin, were not among the aristocratic European-based élite. They were petty colonialists with a difficult position to maintain in a highly stratified, snobbish boom town on the world's frontiers. Their financial status seems to have varied at different times in her life from the reasonably comfortable to the distinctly shabby genteel. In her childhood her father was obliged to take a job, not in the colonial administration which would have been more or less acceptable, but as a manager of one of the Peruvian silver mines. At this point Peru had been conquered by Spain, in the name of Christ, for the exploitation of its mineral wealth (gold and silver) for less than fifty years. ('Why did you come to the New World?' one conquistador was once asked. 'To save souls for God and to get very rich,' was his straightforward answer.) The economic and political complexities of European history which made the brutal exploitation of native South American Indians so attractive to Spain need not be gone into here, but in the silver mines Rose of Lima saw, at first hand, one of the most squalid examples of materialism and petty colonialism, and also one of the most defeated and culturally mutilated people that history offers us. Above all, from her point of view, they had not been converted from their fierce and dangerous gods to the love and freedom that the Holy Catholic Church was supposed to confer. Rose of Lima herself did not write her memoirs, or anything else, so her subjective understanding of this painful phenomenon is not really known; what is known is that she offered her life explicitly for the conversion and salvation of those suffering people – one of the reasons, obviously, why she later seemed an appropriate patron for the New World. (It is simply not true that all Spanish colonialists were brutal, arrogant exploiters of the indigenous peoples; there was a great deal of theological questioning and guilt and struggle around this issue, as the lives of such men as Bartolomé de las Casas makes clear.) Ideas of salvation and conversion were of course inextricably linked in Rose of Lima's culture; and this clear, driving sense of purpose in her life

Through the Devil's Gateway

must not be underestimated if she is to reveal anything to us in a historical sense.

And I think it is very easily underestimated by twentieth-century minds. The temptation to believe that what is most modern is also best – to see human history as a steady progress in knowledge and truth, probably culminating about wherever one happens oneself to be located – has always been almost irresistible, and popularised – if crude – evolutionary theory has, since the last century, added to what seems an historically continual tendency. Its frequency however does not make it right. Believing that people were always like we are, they just didn't understand themselves as well as we do, leads to dangerous historical inaccuracies. Peter Brown in his most recent and profoundly important book *Body and Society*[8] demonstrates movingly how sexuality had so different a social meaning from what it now carries that the sexual abstinences, the noisy and sometimes virulent demands for chastity and virginity, within the early Church, far from being a symptom of self-hatred and dualism, were a radical political claim to the coming of the Kingdom: a claim which women, sometimes even more than men, could make. Likewise Caroline Bynum, in *Holy Feast, Holy Fast*, her book about medieval women religious, pours a rigorous historian's scorn on the idea that the extreme penitential fastings of some of these women can really be diagnosed as anorexic, or as any other sort of neurosis (as proposed for example by Rudolph Bell in *Holy Anorexia*):[9] not merely are the case histories inadequate, but these women's understanding of their bodies, of their relationship to Christ, of their right to participate in his sufferings, of their sense of identity, their very selves, was formed in a social environment so different from our own that nothing is to be gained by reading off their lives in this way rather than exploring in proper detail what it was they did feel and think. She arrives, convincingly, at a much more positive – for the women in question – interpretation; but also one which allows the writings and lives of these women to have a depth and dimension *for us* which was simply not available in many cases while we insisted on trying to see them as sexual victims of appalling restrictions of personal freedom: to see them as though they were us.

Although I do not begin to claim the sort of historical breadth of either Brown or Bynum, I do believe that their approach is not only helpful but necessary if we are going, as we must, to use the lives of women before us to encourage us forward. In the case of Rose of Lima, who is simply a very extreme and therefore very demanding example of a more widespread phenomenon, it seems that we must at least understand, even if we do not wish to reclaim and emulate, the ideas about purity which governed her life. Purity has, rightly, become something of a bugbear to contemporary women: our purity has become men's concern and in its name they have radically restricted our options and liberties. (At a meeting I attended recently about Salman Rushdie's *The Satanic Verses* someone said, 'You do not understand how we have been insulted; it is as though someone had raped my daughter.' This complex linking of women's purity, cultural identity, and religious integrity is something which women obviously need to unknot.) But this idea of 'purity' as something that needs *preserving*, by others, and for others, is quite different from a purity which needs *finding*, indeed which must be searched for, struggled for, hunted down as the precious thing it is. Purity here is not a state of life, an innate condition, but a virtue – something that must be sought, found and won. The etymological connection between 'pure', 'purge' and 'purgatory' becomes clear when the word is understood in this context.

'Blessed are the pure in heart,' the Beatitudes say, 'for they shall see God' (Matt. 5.8). This 'seeing God', a project not just for the afterlife, not just 'jam tomorrow', was the high ambition of anyone who took up a penitential life. Rose of Lima's mystical marriage to Jesus, his visits to her, her direct sense of his immediate and corporeal presence, was understood by her and her contemporaries as a direct reward, and more than a compensation, for the violence of her own purification.

> The Kingdom of heaven is like a merchant in search of fine pearls, who on finding one pearl of great price went and sold all that he had and bought it. (Matt. 13.45–6)

(It is useful to understand here that in the ancient middle east pearls were among the most precious of gems and were highly esteemed as personal ornaments. Hence they are used throughout the Bible, and other classical literature, to represent metaphorically anything of great value, and particularly wise sayings. In medieval Christianity they became more specifically a symbol of purity, not just because of their gentle lustre, but still more because they were grown secretly and, it was believed, *with personal suffering* by the oyster.)

Teilhard de Chardin expressed this understanding of purity not as something passive, but as something both actively gained and worthwhile in itself, in his phrase, 'Purity does not lie in separation from, but in deeper penetration into, the universe.' The problem, particularly for women of such limited resources as Rose of Lima, is how do you, given the restrictions, go about this great work of 'penetrating the universe'?

This image is a particularly appropriate one in Rose of Lima's case. The 'penetration of the universe' in physical terms was going on around her. She was born in Peru less than fifty years after its conquest. The interior of the Americas, beyond the great mountains east of Lima, was still a mystery, but a mystery that brave men were challenging: with immense courage and endurance they set out on travels both dangerous and dazzling. The year she died Sir Walter Raleigh was in South America, on his last ill-fated search for Eldorado: he had, like many of his contemporaries, quite literally put his life on the line to find this worldly paradise. As a child Rose of Lima had watched a different version of the 'penetration of the universe', as the silver mines were sunk deeper and deeper into the mountains, at high risk, in search of treasure.

These brave adventures were only open to men, and their treasure was a worldly one. But the excitement of their explorations, and the promises of hidden treasure to be gained through courage and perseverance, inevitably affected religious language. Both Ignatius of Loyola (1491–1556), the founder of the Jesuits, and Teresa of Avila (1515–82), the radical reformer of the Carmelites, used imagery of exploration and honour to inspire and explain their own radical innovations.

For women who wished to join in this mood of excited expansionist exploration there was an alternative. The exploration could be made into oneself. Caroline Bynum has suggested that the association of women with nature was, at least for thirteenth-century religious, not the negative image that it now seems, but a positive source of spiritual strength and energy.[10] It does not seem wildly improper to apply this to Rose of Lima three hundred years later. Here, on one's own flesh, the universe could be 'penetrated', explored, known, and here the treasure of purity, the pearl of great price, could be discovered. And once discovered could be used to 'buy off' God's justice; could be used to save not only oneself but other suffering souls also.

Rose of Lima left no documentation of her own life. There is no literature or imagery available for analysis. This has however not deterred previous hagiographers. F.M. Capes in *The Flower of the New World* (1899) and F.P. Keyes *The Lily and the Rose* (1962) have sentimentalized her. F.W. Faber seems to have a strangely voyeuristic pleasure in her sufferings. Contemporary feminist writers have seen her rather as a demonstration of the extreme body hatred and guilt that a patriarchal religion lays upon women.[11] All I wish to do here is to suggest that there are other ways of understanding or looking at extremes of penitential life which can suggest in them sources, not of neurotic repression but of freedom and self-ownership.

> **Pure**: Not mixed with anything else; free from adulteration, unimpaired. Without foreign or extraneous admixture; free from anything not properly pertaining to it; homogeneous, unalloyed.[12]

NOTES

1. F.W. Faber, *The Saints and Servants of God*, London, 1847, pp. 27–45 (mine is a minute sampling). Faber's biography of Rose of Lima is in fact a translation and abridgement of J.B. Feuillet's French translation of an Italian text based on original Spanish evidence.
2. What I am trying to say in this essay, could also be applied to a number of other saints, mostly from a slightly earlier, medieval period; and indeed my thinking on this subject has been formed by the historical work of e.g. Caroline Bynum in her book *Holy Feast, Holy Fast* (Berkeley and London, University of California Press, 1987). My selection here of Rose of Lima is quite personal and arises more from work I have been doing on colonialism and religion than any conviction that she is a unique or even a very special case.
3. 'Passionate Prayer: Masochistic Images in women's experience', in Linda Hurcombe (ed.), *Sex and God: Some varieties of women's religious experience*, London, Routledge and Kegan Paul, 1987, pp. 125–40.
4. 'Consolations' is the semi-technical term to describe graces or 'rewards' given by God direct to the aspiring soul.
5. Faber, p. 45.
6. Faber, p. 71.
7. A. Butler, *Lives of the Saints*, 1949 edition, ed. B. Kelly, London, Virtue and Co. Ltd., Vol. III, p. 1056.
8. Peter Brown, *Body and Society*, London, Faber and Faber, 1989.
9. Rudolph M. Bell, *Holy Anorexia*, University of Chicago Press, 1985.

10 Caroline Bynum, 'Women Mystics and Eucharistic Devotion in the thirteenth century', in *Women's Studies II*, Nos 1 & 2, Berkeley, 1984, pp. 179–214.
11 See e.g. my own article cited above in note 3.
12 Oxford English Dictionary.

5 Alison Joseph

The Castration of Women: Nineteenth-century gynaecology and the legacy of biological determinism

In 1896 an American gynaecologist, Dr David Gilliam, wrote that he believed 'That [female] castration pays: that patients are improved, some of them cured, that the moral sense of the patient is elevated, that she becomes tractable, orderly, industrious and cleanly.'[1]

The same man also describes, in his *Text Book of Practical Gynecology (1907)* how such an amputation might be carried out. Here he says that of all cases of hypertrophy of the external genitalia in women, physicians are most frequently consulted regarding the nymphae (the inner labia) and the clitoris, and that the causes of this condition, though not well understood, might be due to 'masturbation, excessive venery, or even the rubbing incident to a pruritis'.[2]

This is not to say that removal of the clitoris was a routine operation either in the States or in Europe at the end of the nineteenth century. However, the enlarged clitoris was a potent symbol within nineteenth-century beliefs on female sexuality and pathology.

Why should the whims of Victorian gynaecology be relevant within a book which discusses the impurity of women in religion? Simply, that the issues that affect our lives are entirely underpinned by a belief in women's dubious nature; their animality, their polluting tendencies, a sense that something might just erupt from the female that is dangerous and needs to be controlled. Medicine is a powerful system of knowledge, and one that affects us all; it is therefore illuminating to find that within modern medical thought these fragments continue to be influential.

In the nineteenth century, it was possible to see female castration as a cure, just as it happens these days that women request cosmetic surgery to make their genitalia look 'more tidy'.[3] In this essay I shall look at the way in which female sexuality has been constructed from a particular biology which has had to exclude female desire. I shall draw from studies of nineteenth-century medicine which show how the Female was defined in certain ways, and I shall look at early psychoanalytic theory in the light of this, to show how the demands of female desire continue to be a problem for modern culture.

Much is made of the distinction between Nature and Culture, and the consequent equation of women with Nature and men with Culture.[4] It seems clearly to describe something about our culture, yet cannot be taken as an absolute. The distinction crystallized in the eighteenth century, at a time when Nature became a category worthy of study, a distinct entity in the projects of the Enlightenment. This coincided with a new urgency to define the differences between men and women, in which the female came to be equated with Nature.[5]

At the same time, there was emerging a new set of theories surrounding reproduction, in which female orgasm was no longer taken for granted as necessary in the conception of a child. A new physical model of the place of male and female in the order of things had emerged. Hippocratic medicine had attributed the inferiority of the female to her being further down the same scale, and simply lacking the necessary heat to become a man. At this time, it was believed that female genitalia were merely internal versions of the male, with the clitoris being a tiny penis, and it was the greater heat of the male that had expelled his organs. This implied that the female contained the potential for being male. This belief continued into the early modern period, when there were celebrated, though rare, cases of pubescent girls becoming boys by a chance generating of sufficient heat.[6]

The same medical model taught that both male and female had to produce the fluids necessary to conceive a child, and it seemed obvious that this occurred, in both sexes, with orgasm.

But by 1800, man and woman were no longer seen as similar bodies on different parts of a scale. As Laqueur says 'By 1800 this view, like that linking female orgasm to conception, had come under devastating attack.'[7] The female body had become a site for intensive study, and there was a new concern to stress its specific femaleness, centred on the uterus. Nineteenth-century medicine debated ovulation and menstruation, its imagination captured by a view of conception wherein the female role was passive and automatic, rather than active and triggered by sexual pleasure. Later in the century, medicine was to apply its expertise to debating whether women really experienced sexual feelings at all.[8]

In the eighteenth century, the category of Nature had acquired a specific importance, yet was also ambivalent. The classical tradition held that Nature became beautiful only when subjected to reason; the romantic view, that Nature was beautiful precisely because she was uncontrolled and was therefore in opposition to Reason. Women, because they were equated with nature, acquired a similar duality, being both repositories of natural laws to be revealed and understood AND the source of uncontrollable passion not tempered by reason and therefore dangerous. Woman as Nature was Other, and one had both to study Her and unearth the laws of nature which She contained, and also attempt to restrain the potentially dangerous powers She possessed.[9]

If woman was Other, this process of discovery and restraint was thought of as something carried out by men. As Jordanova says, 'Science and Medicine as activities were associated with sexual metaphors which were clearly expressed in designating nature as a woman to be unveiled, unclothed and penetrated by Masculine Science.'[10] Jordanova goes on to describe the statue in the Paris medical faculty, which shows a young woman, with bare breasts, head bowed, in the process of removing her veil: it is called 'Nature unveils herself before Science'.

As this conception of medical activity was carried into the nineteenth century, so did the changing medical model in some way foster the quest for truth in bodies. The domestic medicine of the eighteenth century had seen disease as an imbalance of humours, with the body a system of interrelated organs and parts. In the nineteenth century, disease itself came to be the object of investigation, and diseases came to be located in specific parts of the body. The science of physiology emerged, and pathological anatomy grew in status to become a keystone of medical practice.

The dissection of human rather than animal corpses became important to this new status. In the late eighteenth and early nineteenth centuries, medical teaching began to use wax anatomical models, moulded from dissected human corpses.[11] One of the most significant collections of these models is at the Museo

'La Specola', at the University of Florence, where life-size models created in the late eighteenth and early nineteenth century are on display. Both male and female bodies have been used, and it is striking how art and anatomy combine inextricably in the way they are posed. The males, although stripped of skin, are often leaning on an elbow in a classical pose. Most of the female figures have only their abdomen dissected, the rest of the body, with milky white skin and beautiful hair, reclining in a pose from a classical aesthetic of the female. There are many reasons why, in the early nineteenth century, different considerations would intrude on the modelling of a dissected female body rather than that of a male, but one conclusion we could draw from these figures is that the human norm is male, and the only reason to look at female bodies is for that which makes them female, i.e. the reproductive system.

To look at them now, they seem eloquent, somehow symbolic, of the ideas surrounding their creation: aesthetic, yet dissected, sexual yet grotesque. Jordanova suggests that the search to define femininity by recourse to anatomy was a search for aesthetic and moral ideals at the same time; she says of these models, 'The figures of recumbent women seem to convey for the first time the sexual potential of medical anatomy.'[12]

Jules Michelet, writing his book on *Woman* (1859, Paris), part of his works on Natural History, turned first to the dissecting room. He believed that women are to be adored for their naturalness, but because this makes them vulnerable and subject to extremes of temperament, they should also be under the control of their husbands.[13]

All this gave rise to insoluble contradictions; women were closer to nature, which was a benign being, and therefore could be a source of purity and balance; women were animal and brutish, compared to the civilized potential of the male. Women could reveal the laws of nature, if (male) science developed the tools to understand her; women, being natural, were the source of terrible passions, and less able to be tempered by reason.

The debate regarding ovulation, therefore, resonated within an episteme that came to regard the female as a passive, potentially dangerous source of raw passion. And within this, therefore, female sexual desire was a problem for nineteenth-century medicine. Discussion centred on the discovery that ovulation was an automatic, monthly occurrence. But confusion reigned over the idea of the menstrual cycle. In 1844, a London surgeon, G.F. Girdwood, wrote an article in *The Lancet* which, based on his extensive zoological studies of dogs and horses, showed that menstruation was the human version of being 'on heat' – it showed the readiness of the female for impregnation. Girdwood's essay was in response to those who believed menstruation to be a peculiarly human phenomenon. Of interest to us, however, is his attempt to address the question why, if the time of bleeding is the most fertile time, do women tend to shun male company just at this part of the cycle? He answers:

> 'Her social position has rendered woman keenly percipient of every thought and action beautiful or graceful, . . . taught from infancy to subjugate her passions and affections, her thoughts, her looks, her language kept under control . . . Need it be a matter of wonder, when we see her capable of such restraint in general, that she should retire within herself and exercise that control we find her continually exerting over all her thoughts and actions the more energetically at a time when she is taught that a stray thought of desire would be impurity and its fruition pollution. To aid her in such a duty Nature has wisely provided her with the sexual appetite slightly developed'.[14]

It is of interest that he notes the reader may be 'startled' by this last assertion.

It seems that a new vocabulary was emerging for describing the physical events of women's lives. Thomas Laqueur quotes various nineteenth-century writers who use metaphors of enlargement, bursting and rupture; words such as 'rut', previously applied only to dogs, were employed to describe women. Havelock Ellis said, 'A worm gnaws periodically at the roots of women's life.' Walter Heape, a reader in zoology and an anti-suffragist, writing at the end of the century, exulted in a description of menstruation which wallowed in gore, a picture of devastation, rupture, torn membranes, 'from which it would hardly seem possible to heal satisfactorily without the aid of surgical treatment' . . .[15]

There also continued to be a confusion between menstruation and its connection with sexual feelings. As described by Girdwood, in the terrible time of menstruation, the inner rupture and tearing have to be transcended by female calm and restraint. This terminology borrowed directly from ideas of female passion, which also used a language of seething emotions having to be restrained by modesty. Women, being closer to nature because of their biology, were more likely to be overcome by powerful feelings, and the burden therefore fell upon women to control themselves, for their good and for the good of all around them.

In this sense of lurking danger associated with women's physical nature, there came to be linked with the female an idea of innate pathology. (This was not new; Hippocrates is supposed to have said 'What is Woman? Disease!'[16]) It is in Michel Foucault that we can find a broader view of the place of the pathological female in the modern medical paradigm. In *The History of Sexuality* he describes how modern western culture has developed, uniquely, a *scientia sexualis:* 'procedures for telling the truth of sex which are geared to a form of knowledge-power.'[17]

Medicine, according to Foucault, is a key institution in the creation of specific mechanisms of knowledge and power centring on sex. Foucault maintains that nineteenth-century medicine defined four 'privileged objects of knowledge' – that is, four problematized areas whose cross-examination would reveal truths: the hysterical woman, the masturbating child, the couple who practised birth control and the perverse adult.[18]

He describes the 'hysterization of women's bodies',

> whereby the feminine body was analyzed ... as being thoroughly saturated with sexuality; whereby it was integrated into the sphere of medical practices, by reason of a pathology intrinsic to it; whereby, finally, it was placed in organic communication with the social body, whose regulated fecundity it was supposed to ensure ... the Mother, with her negative image of 'nervous woman', constituted the most visible form of this hysterization.[19]

In the nineteenth-century, the pathology of the female came to be focused upon the hysteric. There was a general view that all women held within them the potential to become hysterical; from 'nervous' to 'hysteric' to insane was a sliding scale, and all women were positioned somewhere upon it. This is very clearly exposed in the debate surrounding the use of chloroform as an anaesthetic, which emerged in the middle years of the nineteenth century. Its use for childbirth was the focus of great controversy, which itself sheds light on the contradictions surrounding the idea of the female. Mary Poovey[20] examines the questions at the heart of the debate: Is the woman in labour outside man's intervention i.e. if God had cursed Eve with painful childbirth, is it up to man to lift that curse? This resounds with the buzz of contradictory definitions of the female as being natural or subject to cultural intervention. More importantly for this essay, Poovey shows how the debate happened around the prone body of the silenced, anaesthetized woman: and how the body itself, now the repository, in a way, of Desire itself, came to behave accordingly.

Poovey cites numerous articles describing the sexual and hysterical behaviour of women under the influence of anaesthetic. An article by W. Tyler Smith in *The Lancet* in 1847 described a woman under the influence of chloroform trying to kiss an attendant. It becomes an argument about propriety: Smith says 'May it not be that in woman the physical pain neutralizes the sexual emotions which would otherwise . . . tend very much to alter our estimation of the modesty and retiredness proper to the sex, and which are never more prominent or more admirable than on these occasions?'[21] Note that it is a problem for the doctor first and foremost.

There is a generally accepted view that people 'going under' anaesthetic do display extremes of behaviour – but here it was viewed automatically as sexual, as if the expectations of the doctors did not allow for anything else. (Similar behaviour by men was viewed as belligerent rather than sexual.)

Interestingly, Dr James Young Simpson of Edinburgh University, who was one of the first to use chloroform, flatly denied any of these side effects, and said the doctors were seeing what they wanted to see. But as Poovey points out, men on both sides of the dispute were agreed as to the basic nature of women: the question was whether chloroform should be allowed to tamper with it.

This was all the more prominent in operations rather than in childbirth. Smith described an operation to remove 'enlarged nymphae' where the patient behaved in a sexual way. According to Dr Tanner in *The Lancet* of 1849, ether used in an operation on the vagina of a prostitute incited 'lascivious dreams'.[22]

Poovey describes the silenced female body as a site upon which men can inscribe their anxieties about their sexuality and that of women.

By the end of the nineteenth-century, the biological model of sexuality was so constructed that it had become perfectly coherent to argue that excessive sexual desire in a woman was pathological. For the female, the whole mechanism of reproduction was now viewed as automatic, a passive and intrinsic part of woman's nature. Given this, the clitoris was rather a problem, because to argue from biology and physiology gave one no defence against the fact that the clitoris was the female organ of pleasure.

The potency of the clitoris as a symbol in the nineteenth century is well documented. For example, regarding prostitutes, the most crucially sexualized women of the time, questions were asked concerning the size of their genitalia, and various medical projects were embarked upon to prove that an enlarged clitoris was a sign of a tendency to prostitution (in the same way that phrenologists were measuring criminals' heads). Such studies were inconclusive, but this in no way diminished the influence of the idea that excessive sexual urges in a woman would be linked to the size of her clitoris. In fact, nineteenth century pornography contains examples of one woman making love to another using her huge clitoris as a penis.[23]

If the 'normal' woman had no libido, our worthy surgeons had to do something about the clitoris. Cutting it off was the most simple expedient – and indeed, the effect was to cure the patient of that pathological and dangerous state – sexual desire.

In the transition from the nineteenth century to the twentieth century, clitoridectomy, it appears, ceased to be acceptable. In this transition it became metaphorical rather than actual. Sigmund Freud had completed his medical training in the nineteenth century. He believed in biology (in *Beyond the Pleasure Principle* he says, 'Biology is truly a land of unlimited possibilities.'[24]), he had studied hysteria, and his views on sexuality have set the agenda for much of our century. As for Freud, the clitoris continues to be surrounded by the same problems that it held for nineteenth-century medicine. For him, the auto-erotic experiences of little boys or girls are not very different, as boys find their pleasure from their penis, girls from the clitoris. But from this he suggests 'that the sexuality of little girls is of a wholly masculine character.' He goes on to say:

> Indeed, if we were able to give a more definite connotation to the concepts of 'masculine' and 'feminine', it would even be possible to maintain the libido is invariably and necessarily of a masculine nature, whether it occurs in men or in women.[25]

Elsewhere he describes women as having an essentially passive sexual function, '... so that its course is determined by the treatment accorded by the man.'[26]

In the Freudian view of the development of the little girl, the clitoris is the centre of her infantile pleasure, until she realizes that it can never be a penis and must transfer her sexual centre to her vagina. According to Freud, this happens after a period of 'anaesthesia', in fact, often not until after first coitus. Frigidity becomes the spectre hovering over this transition, should it not be properly accomplished, and the frigid woman was one who had failed to make this transference. Freud says, 'In those women who are sexually anaesthetic as it is called, the clitoris has stubbornly retained this sensitivity.'[27]

Even the process of normal development required something of self-sacrifice about it, as women learned that instead of their early pleasures they must be content with the possibility of having a child. In 1930, Helene Deutsch described the syndrome of frigidity in a significant group of her patients, women who are 'psychically healthy', yet for whom the concept of orgasm was completely alien: 'In intercourse they experience a happy and tender sense that they are giving keen pleasure, convinced that coitus is of importance only to the man. In it, as in other relations, the woman finds happiness in tender, maternal giving.'[28]

Whatever the status of this piece of research in modern psychoanalysis, it needs only a cursory glance at the problem pages of women's magazines, particularly those for an older readership, to find that this syndrome of the woman who considers herself happily married, yet is bewildered by the concept of orgasm which she herself has never experienced, is still familiar. Our Victorian legacy means that we have no access to the vocabulary of desire. How can women who have been taught that their choice in sexual relations is passive, limited to being able to say yes or no when approached by a man, be expected to make a sudden leap into active love-making where their desire is acknowledged, and their pleasure is a definite goal? Indeed, the idea that women might take control of their desire to the point where men come to be judged as objects of pleasure is felt to be so threatening as to be tabooed. (It is in lesbian writing that one finds a sense of what might be possible if women's desire was autonomous and acknowledged.)

If we return to Deutsch, writing more than fifty years ago, she adds: 'This type of woman is dying out, and the modern woman seems to be neurotic if she is frigid . . .'

Now, it is true that the concept of frigidity has lost its urgency in these liberated times when orgasm is every woman's right. But one might also ask, why is the idea of faking orgasm, which ought to be nonsense, still given space in modern and sophisticated women's magazines?

Significantly, Deutsch adds:

> ... I think that this psychological change is in accordance with social developments and that it is accompanied by an increasing tendency of women towards masculinity. Perhaps the women of the next generation will no longer submit to defloration in the normal way and will give birth to children only on condition of freedom from pain...'[29]

Deutsch believed that masochism was 'the most elementary force in feminine mental life'. Acceptance of pain was the bridge that enabled a girl to relinquish her hope that her clitoris would become a penis, and to become instead a mature woman whose sexuality was focused upon her vagina.

We are the women of the next generation; and, yes, we do refuse to submit to 'defloration in the normal way'. But can we really dismiss Deutsch's proscriptive view of our biological masochism, strange as it is? When women describe their sexual fantasies, they tend to depict women suffering various degrees of powerlessness, humiliation or pain, similar to those fantasies described by men. It seems to be the case that we interweave desire and pleasure with pain and punishment; that for women, the chasing of elusive sexual goals remains familiar, and our pleasure is indeed obscured behind a barbed wire fence of masochistic images.[30]

The science of biology, therefore, has had a profound effect on how we view our sexual identity. Nineteenth-century feminism had no desire at all to reject biological determinism; and I would argue that even today, it would take a leap of imagination to put anything in its place.

In the nineteenth century, biology had split sex from reproduction. And indeed, feminism was quite happy with that, for it heralded a new way of being. One could calmly ovulate and not even know one was doing it, as it all happened 'down there'; this left 'up here' free for intellectual thought. Women now had a position from which to fight off ideas of wild passions and uncontrollable desires; indeed, in doing so they could claim the higher moral ground for themselves, supported by all sorts of biological arguments concerning their greater gentleness and delicacy.

As Thomas Laqueur says:

> In these new discursive wars, feminism as well as anti-feminism sacrificed the idea of women as inherently passionate; sexual pleasure as a sign in the flesh of reproductive capacity fell victim to political exigencies.[31]

This was not altogether without a sense of loss, from those individuals, perhaps, who believed passion to be vital and life-affirming. There is a scene in H.G. Wells's novel *Ann Veronica* (1909), where Ann, the rebellious young woman who has left suburban tedium for a London life as a New Woman and student of biology, discusses Love, in particular, physical love, with a keen Fabian Socialist and Suffragette, Miss Miniver:

> 'Don't we all rather humbug about the coarseness? All we women, I mean,' said [Ann]. She decided to go on, after a momentary halt. 'We pretend bodies are ugly. Really they are the most beautiful things in the world. We pretend that we never think of everything that makes us what we are.'
> 'No,' cried Miss Miniver almost vehemently. 'You are wrong! I did not think you thought such things. Bodies! Bodies! horrible things! We are souls. Love lives on a higher plane. We are not animals. If ever I did meet a man I could love, I should love him' – her voice dropped again – 'Platonically' . . .
> She turned her face to the fire, gripped her hands upon her elbows, and drew her thin shoulders together in a shrug. 'Ugh!' she said.[32]

Of course, for every Miss Miniver of 1909 there was probably an Ann Veronica, her dormant and delicious sexuality just waiting for H. G. Wells, New Man that he was, to wave his magic wand. But Ann Veronica's slow awakening, albeit eighty years ago, is not so unfamiliar to us now, when there is a sense that our own desire, our own pleasure, is something for which we have to struggle.

Foucault describes how we are living in a world of endless insatiable chatter about sex which feeds on the illusion that if we question Sex enough it will reveal its Truths. And yet, surely, certain voices must be raised, must rise above the hubbub, if, as Foucault himself says, 'We aim through a tactical reversal of the various mechanisms of sexuality to counter the grips of power with the claims of bodies, pleasures and knowledges, in their multiplicity and their possibility of resistance. The rallying point for the counter-attack against the deployment of sexuality ought not to be sex-desire but bodies and pleasures.'[33]

In my biology lessons at school we were told that humans are the only mammals available for sex the whole time. But most *male* mammals *are* ready for sex the whole time. It is the females who come on heat and who therefore determine when sex takes place. My point is not to argue about the sex life of the marmoset. It is that to a class of fifteen-year-olds in a co-ed comprehensive school, such a statement told us something influential about the culture in which we were growing up and nothing about gerbils. It would have been more helpful, perhaps, to have had it put another way, for example, that humans are the only mammalian group where the rhythms of the female are systematically overridden by the male.

Of course, we'd have learnt that anyway. We have had no choice but to take on board a sexuality which is defined in terms of its difference from the male, and therefore mystified; which has been derived from biology and based around reproduction. For the biological model of the nineteenth century has never been replaced. Medicine continues to be a very powerful system of knowledge, and although there are many differences between nineteenth century and twentieth century medicine, there is still at its heart a view of the body (both male and female) as a repository for disease.

Women continue to be defined by a passive and automatic reproductive cycle, and sex continues to be determined by male desire and female consent (and sometimes even that isn't necessary). Where desire has been returned to us, it is in the shape of a 'masculine' libido which fits us very badly, and even then we have no vocabulary with which to express it. A wolf-whistle from a man indicates an active desire. From a woman, it can at most indicate availability. Pictures of naked women are testimony to the power that is maintained by men while the erotic 'gaze' is one-way. When we can look upon a man in the same way (not that this is necessarily desirable) then the world will have changed.

And this is why we still carry the burden of having to control the chaos that might break forth should we allow those troubled depths of tempestuous passion to break the surface calm of 'normal' desire. The madness of all this is constantly illustrated by a jumbled host of fragmentary images that surround us, of body hair and smells and leakings, of panty liners, bikini lines and cellulite.

Our bodies are problems. We are told by medicine, by advertising, by the fashion and cosmetics industry, that it is so, and we believe it. We suffer 'those difficult days', we fear being too hairy, or too smelly. We give birth surrounded by people who reflect our own fear that we will lose control and that our animal self will burst forth noisily and messily. We expend endless energy and an awful lot of time each day in pre-empting criticism; in censoring our speech and our behaviour, checking our appearance, taking up less room, making ourselves invisible, smiling at the request of total strangers, feigning pleasure when we feel none – being good girls rather than real women. And it seems to me, we must closely examine the roots of all this before we can begin to think how it could be otherwise. For we still believe that our femaleness is a biological entity; but it is this biology that a century ago wished to remove our clitoris and that continues now to impose upon us a desire that only functions in passive reaction to the actions of men, and that is as a result based in narcissism and masochism.

Without disentangling the threads of the web that surrounds us, any attempt to describe how things might be otherwise will fail. It has been fashionable in the last twenty years to suggest that there was in ancient history a utopian matriarchy. There may well have been, but an examination of those described shows the limitations of biological determinism.

Elizabeth Gould Davies in *The First Sex*[34], describes the great ancient civilizations of Crete, Egypt and Sumer, which were ruled by women, who had instituted an incest taboo and exogamy to control 'the lusts of their sons'. The innate moral superiority of women (given their basic nature) meant that all was harmony. But then the disenfranchised men waged war and the ensuing chaos is with us still. We are back with Miss Miniver, her glasses glinting in the firelight.

It may well be the case that a social system organized by women would be wonderful, that there would be no war because we wouldn't have our children killed, that there would be communes and free child care and no VAT on sanitary protection . . . but how would we ever know? How do we know it wouldn't be a place of savagery and high priestesses and the ritual sacrifice of beautiful twelve-year-old boys?

Biology offers another alternative, in the form of Mary Jane Sherfey, an American psychiatrist. She has studied extensively within anatomy and endocrinology, and argues that from life in the womb onwards, the female is the basic sex. Quoting Masters and Johnson on the similarity of the orgasm in men and women, she puts paid to that old Freudian idea of an infantile clitoral orgasm versus a mature vaginal one; and concludes triumphantly that male and female genitalia are not very different. 'Our myth of the female's relative asexuality is a biological absurdity,' she says.[35] So biology has returned to us our castrated clitoris – but accompanied by a health warning. She continues:

> It is conceivable that the forceful suppression of women's inordinate sexual demands was a pre-requisite to the dawn of every modern civilization, and almost every human culture. Primitive woman's drive was too strong, too susceptible to the fluctuating extremes of an impelling, aggressive erotism to withstand the disciplined requirements of a settled family life...[36]

Whilst we believe in our biologically-determined nature, there will be no possible utopia apart from these two: a matriarchy run by morally superior women, where desire is excluded, and where our innate niceness means that we can all live happily ever after; or, we let the chaos out, and we rule fiercely and savagely for a short-lived reign, our ferocious and insatiable desire destroying everything around us. This is the dual nature of woman epitomized in nineteenth-century medical beliefs and which continues today.

When Foucault talks of a sexuality defined by 'bodies and pleasures' he simply must be heard. The powerful multiplicity of sexuality has for too long been reduced to the level of the coarse car sticker, the symbol of two feet pointing upwards and two feet pointing downwards. It is a dangerous impoverishment, which, when fed upon by insatiable economic forces, results in its own logical conclusions of snuff movies and child pornography. There has to be a new definition of sexuality: nurtured by everyday physical experience rather than separate from it, revered for its danger yet ribald and jolly, both everyday and sacramental. It is not just that things could be other than they are – it is that they must be.

NOTES

1 Dr David Gilliam, 1896, quoted in Robert S. Mendelsohn, *Male Practice: How Doctors Manipulate Women* (Chicago, Contemporary Books, 1981), pp. 30–31.
2 David Gilliam, *A Text Book of Practical Gynecology* (Philadelphia 1907), p. 84
3 My evidence for this, as for many of the intimate facts of women's lives, is anecdotal, gathered from women of my own acquaintance.
4 See the essay by Leonie J. Archer in this book.
5 See L.J. Jordanova, 'Natural Facts: a historical perspective on Science and Sexuality' in Carol P. McCormack and Marilyn Strathearn (eds), *Nature, Culture and Gender* (Cambridge University Press, 1980), pp. 42–69.
6 One of the best examples is in Ambroise Paré, *Des Monstres et Prodigues*, (1573). This is quoted in Thomas Laqueur, 'Orgasm, Generation and the Politics of Reproductive Biology' in Gallagher, Laqueur (eds), *The Making of the Modern Body*, University of California Press, 1987.
7 Laqueur, p. 2
8 There are various examples of this in nineteenth-century medical writings. See William Acton, *The Functions and Disorders of the Reproductive Organs*, 6th ed, London, 1875.
9 See Thomas L. Hankins, *Science and the Enlightenment* (Cambridge University Press, 1985), p. 5.
10 Jordanova, p. 45.
11 Examples of wax anatomy models can be seen at the Wellcome Collections, The Science Museum, London.
12 Jordanova, p. 54.
13 Jules Michelet, *La Femme*, Paris, Hachette, 1860; quoted in Jordanova, pp. 57, 62.
14 G.F. Girdwood, in *The London Lancet*, 30 November 1844.
15 Laqueur, pp. 31–32. Heape quoted from 1894.
16 Quoted from Mary Poovey (see below) in a footnote, p. 163.
17 Michel Foucault, *The History of Sexuality, an Introduction*, trans. Robert Hurley (Harmondsworth, Penguin, 1984), p. 58.
18 Foucault, p. 105.
19 Foucault, p. 104.
20 Mary Poovey, 'Scenes of an Indelicate Character: the medical treatment of Victorian Women' in Gallagher and Laqueur, *The Making of the Modern Body*, pp. 137–68.
21 Poovey, p. 143.
22 Poovey, p. 144.
23 For more on the classification of prostitutes, see Sander Gilman, 'Black Bodies, White Bodies – towards an iconography of female sexuality in late 19th century art, medicine and literature', in *Critical Inquiry*, no. 12, vol. 1, (Autumn 1985), p. 204. For more on Victorian

pornography, see Steven Marcus, *The Other Victorians – A study of Sexuality and Pornography in Mid-19th century England*, London, Weidenfeld and Nicholson, 1966.
24 Sigmund Freud, *Beyond the Pleasure Principle*, London, 1920, quoted by Mary Jane Sherfey, *The Nature and Evolution of Female Sexuality*, (New York, Random House, 1972), p. ix.
25 Sigmund Freud, *Three Essays on Sexuality*, Standard edition of the Complete Works, vol. 7 (London, Hogarth Press, 1953), Essay III, 'Puberty', pp. 219–20.
26 Sigmund Freud, *Introductory Lectures on Psychoanalysis* (London, 1922), lecture 25, p. 335.
27 Freud, ibid, lecture 20, p. 267.
28 Helene Deutsch, 'The Significance of Masochism in the Mental Life of Women', 1930, reprinted in Robert Fliess (ed.) *The Psychoanalytic Reader*, London, Hogarth Press, 1950.
29 ibid.
30 One of the key works on women's sexual fantasies is Nancy Friday, *My Secret Garden*, London, Quartet, 1975.
31 Laqueur, p. 35.
32 H.G. Wells, *Ann Veronica* (London, Virago, 1980), p. 144.
33 Foucault, p. 157.
34 Elizabeth Gould Davis, *The First Sex*, New York, G. P. Putnam, 1971, quoted by Paula Webster in her essay 'A Vision of Power' in Rayna Rapp Reiter (ed.), *Towards an Anthropology of Women* (New York Monthly Review Press, 1975), p. 152.
35 Mary Jane Sherfey, *The Nature and Evolution of Female Sexuality* (New York, 1972), p. 113.
36 Sherfey, p. 138.

Linda Sireling

6

The Jewish Woman: Different and Equal

When I was much younger, and not as religious as I am today, I thought that religious Jews had sex through a hole in a sheet, wore clothes from the last century, and were generally out of touch with life and the world we live in. Now I am thirty-five years old, and married to a traditional observant Jew and living in one of London's most Jewish areas, I can laugh at the mistaken ideas I had. In this chapter, I would like to try to explain some of the laws and customs of my people, particularly with regard to women and marriage, and dispel some of the myths and fairy stories which had totally misled me.

I always thought that to be a religious Jew, you had to dress like someone from nineteenth-century Poland. I now realize that there are different kinds of Jews, ranging from the ultra-religious Chasidim who do dress like that, to Liberal Jews who do not recognize the holy nature of the Bible and who prefer to keep whichever laws they can rationalize. There are also many Jews in between who dress modestly and where possible in the latest fashions, and who keep the laws of the Bible without losing touch with the world we live in. The women go out to work in the same way as other women, but know that their main priority in life is to care for their families. They are not in any way second class citizens.

For the main misconception that many people have is that orthodox women are regarded as inferior to men. There are various reasons for this misconception; men are obliged to pray three times a day, and women are exempt from time-related duties, possibly because their loyalties would conflict with running a home and looking after children. Of course women are biologically different from men, and the roles for women and men are clearly defined in Jewish law. In the synagogue, men can be called to the reading of the Bible, whereas the women cannot, and the sexes are separated. The reason for keeping women and men separated is that it is felt that a man cannot concentrate on prayer when women are in close proximity. Judaism recognizes the tremendous power of women's sexuality, and it is the acknowledgement of this power that is at the heart of many of the Jewish laws concerning women's lives.

The Jewish law regarding sexual relations is not at all related to the Christian concept of sex being sin, or to women being sinful in some way. The power of a woman's sexuality is very strong and the orthodox woman must take responsibility for that. She must not only dress modestly, but behave modestly as well. Modest dress means that hemlines must be below the knee, and sleeves below the elbow. Necklines cannot be low-cut, and see-through blouses are definitely not allowed! An orthodox man is not allowed to hear a woman singing as this is felt to be seductive. It is also considered indecent for couples to be seen to be intimate in public because sex should be a private affair, only between man and wife. Cuddling on the couch with your husband in front of other people is frowned upon just as much as kissing him in the street. The obligation of modesty is on both men and women; men are also required to dress and behave in a modest way.

Modesty in looks and behaviour is considered to be the ideal in Judaism. A woman should never flirt with a man other than her husband, but this does not mean that she is oppressed in any way. In fact, many women feel that *tzniut*, or modesty, is not only a protection for her which serves as a 'hands off' signal to men, but also allows a responsibility for her own actions. She is released from being a sex object, unlike most women in the secular western world, from being a rival for the latest cover on *Cosmopolitan*. I find that many great orthodox women have an aura of confidence about them, in contrast to the way the media give conflicting and undermining messages about the ideal woman. After all, most women do not look like cover girls, and the Jewish woman is free to be beautiful in an inner way, not as a clone of an advertisement.

All the Jewish laws are derived from the first five books of the Old Testament, or what Jewish people refer to as the Torah, or the five books of Moses; we believe that these laws were given by God to the Jewish people. The laws are central to our way of life: their structure is rigid. At first glance they may seem confining and restrictive, but more careful evaluation shows that the structure of laws enables us to live in a healthy and balanced way, in moderation and without excess. Judaism is a practical religion, with practical solutions, where actions speak louder than words. Judaism affects every sphere of life: eating, drinking, talking, praying, conducting business – the list is endless. The rabbi's role is primarily as a teacher, not like a priest who might mediate between the individual and God. The individual Jew must make his own pact with the Almighty, and pray directly to Him, not through an agent. Most people do not realize that Jews can pray together without a rabbi, and that the rabbi's job is often to clarify a point of law or resolve a dispute, rather than to lead a congregation in prayer.

The Torah is the basis for all the Jewish laws and our moral code and our laws come from this. There are many stories in the Bible about great love between men and women, but the ideal role models in Judaism are considered to be the Patriarchs and Matriarchs: Sarah and Abraham, Isaac and Rebecca, and Jacob and Rachel. The relationship between husband and wife is seen as the closest one can get to God; the love that a man and woman feel for each other is the highest form of spirituality.

The thread of love running through the story of Sarah and Abraham illustrates the partnership between the couple. The Jewish commentaries on the story tell of how the two of them worked as a team, educating the people around them, teaching them that they should not worship idols, and that there is only one God. Abraham taught the men, while Sarah taught the women. In prophecy, Sarah was equal to Abraham, and in a certain instance Abraham was told by God to listen to his wife Sarah. The story of Jacob and Rachel illustrates the love of a man for a woman, a love which is human and normal, but based on heavenly values, on giving rather than taking. Jacob saw something in Rachel that was very special, and he loved her in the true sense of the word; the word 'love' in Hebrew, which is the original language of the Bible, comes from the root of the word meaning 'to give', or 'to want to give'. The ideal love of a man for a woman and of a woman for a man is for them to want to give something to each other, or to want to do something for each other.

The main area of confusion with regard to the Jewish attitude to women concerns the laws of marriage, particularly in respect of menstruation and childbirth. These laws are called *Taharat HaMishpachah*, the laws of family purity. The verse in the Bible which has been most misquoted and misunderstood is Leviticus 15.19, which says: 'And if a woman have an issue, and her issue in her flesh be blood, she shall be in her impurity seven days; and whosoever toucheth her shall be unclean until the even.'

To take this law out of context is very misleading. It is not true to say that a menstruating woman is unclean – she has a status of *tameh*, a word which has been wrongly translated for years as 'unclean' but which would be much better translated as 'impure'. A woman who was menstruating was not allowed into the Temple. There are many reasons for these laws; some are obvious, but some are very deep and one level of understanding is that menstruation represents a loss of potential life; the same applied to a man who had a nocturnal emission, or wet dream, or someone who had helped to prepare a body for burial. Such men and women were only permitted to enter the Temple after they had purified themselves in a special ritual bath, a specifically constructed natural gathering of water. This is often misunderstood as cleaning oneself of contamination, but is obviously not the case as is proven by the fact that they had to clean themselves carefully before going into the bath, or *mikva* as it is called, so it becomes clear that it was to purify themselves spiritually, not physically.

Whenever a person is confronted either with death or potential life, they must immerse themselves in a *mikva* in order to purify themselves spiritually. Although the Temple was destroyed two thousand years ago, Jews hope that one day the Messiah will come, the Temple will be rebuilt, and Jews will be spiritually pure again. But until that time comes, we can only keep the laws relating to spiritual purity which are unconnected with the Temple. Marriage in Judaism is of such a high status that when a Jewish couple are married, it is considered that the home is like a small version of the Temple and spirituality is brought to everyday life by keeping the biblical laws.

Rabbi Arye Kaplan, in his book *Waters of Eden* (New York, NCSY/Orthodox Union, 1976) discusses the significance of water being used for purification. Natural rain water is an essential part of spiritual purification because of the link with the original water created in the Garden of Eden (Gen. 2.10: 'And a river went out of Eden to water the Garden ...'). Adam lost his spiritual purity through eating the forbidden fruit, so God gave him the opportunity to reinstate himself partially through immersion in the original water which came from Eden. Although while we are alive we can never return to Eden, we can benefit from the ever-flowing waters of Eden. Water, the original substance which God created when he made the world, represents change, and immersing oneself in a natural body of water is the only way of changing one's spiritual identity. In the same way that man cannot live under water, so while people are totally immersed in the water, it is as if they are dead. When they come out of the water, it is as if the *mikva* represents the womb and they are reborn.

When a woman has finished her menstrual period and has counted seven days when no fresh bleeding has been apparent, she must immerse herself in a *mikva* before sexual relations with her husband can resume. For all the days before her visit to the *mikva* she is *nidda*, or set apart, and she and her husband must not even touch.

A bride must immerse herself in a *mikva* before her wedding. The men amongst the ultra-religious Chasidim immerse themselves in a *mikva* before the onset of the sabbath in order to purify themselves spiritually. A woman who has given birth must immerse herself in a *mikva* before she can resume sexual relations with her husband. A convert to Judaism has to immerse him or herself in a *mikva*. *Mikva* represents a change in status.

Sex in Judaism is not only for procreation, although of course that is very important. Sex is pleasurable and is meant to be so. Anything else would be unnatural. Jewish law teaches us that sex is equally important between a married couple who wish to have children and between a couple where the woman may be infertile or menopausal. However, there are limitations because Judaism is a moral code, from which some more recent religions such as Christianity stem. Sexual deviations are forbidden to preserve a healthy society.

A husband and wife must be faithful to one another, and divorce is used as a last resort if the relationship breaks down. A man must divorce his wife if he cannot get on with her; she has a right to petition for divorce if he refuses to have sex with her. The husband has an obligation to satisfy his wife in bed, and the rabbis have written about this in the Talmud, the Jewish law books.

Through the Devil's Gateway

Before my marriage, I had to arrange a visit to the *mikva*. I was not from a religious background, and I had previously thought that anyone who went to the *mikva* had to wear ghastly old-fashioned dresses with thick tights and live in a Yiddish-speaking ghetto! My mother and my best friend, both of whom believed that I could just as well have a bath at home, came with me. We were all very surprised to see the modern bathrooms, and tasteful surroundings, as well as meeting the *mikva* attendant who not only spoke English, but was very friendly and helpful as well. It is customary for a bride to be accompanied to the *mikva*, usually by her mother, but after the wedding, any future visits are on one's own because of the principles of modesty. I prepared myself for immersion, with my new book of instructions at hand, and then went down the steps of the *mikva* into the water, with my mother and friend and the attendant watching me. When I came out of the water, they all had tears in their eyes.

To understand the concept of *mikva*, it may be helpful to picture it. The *mikva* itself is a collection of natural water, which looks a bit like a small swimming pool. There are steps leading down so that you can stand up to about chest-level in water, and there are radiators at the sides of the bath to heat the water to a pleasant temperature. Immersion is at nightfall. This is because that is the beginning of the Jewish day: 'and there was evening and there was morning, one day' (Gen. 1.5). Before entering the *mikva*, you take a bath, cut your finger- and toe-nails, comb your hair thoroughly and make sure that every part of you is scrupulously clean. The immersion in the *mikva* is only valid if there is no obstruction between the body and the water, and this means that you have to take off your jewellery, glasses, contact lenses, nail varnish, make up and elastoplast, in fact anything which forms a barrier between yourself and the water. The *mikva* attendant must always be there to make sure that every hair on your head is totally immersed in the water, so when you are ready, you call her and then make your descent into the *mikva*. When I go, I hold my breath and completely immerse myself under the water, trying to keep as relaxed as possible, and I stay under the water for a few seconds. Sometimes I try to think about the concepts behind the immersion and about being spiritually cleansed, and sometimes *mikva* is just something that has to be done on time, and the spiritual significance is almost forgotten in the ritual of the act. I then have to say the blessing in Hebrew followed by two more quick dips under the water and out into my lovely warm soft towel!

I tend to take the beautiful surroundings of the *mikva* for granted; in my local *mikva*, the private bathrooms which lead in total privacy into one of two *mikvas* are beautifully decorated and colour co-ordinated, centrally heated with modern power-showers and flouncy floral curtains all around. The *mikva* is situated in an out-building in the synagogue grounds, and there is a car park outside. I also take for granted the fact that the water is normally heated, and that there is a *mikva* which is easily accessible from my home. The Bible laws of *mikva* are so important for women, that women have gone to extraordinary lengths to keep them. It is really very easy for people like me, in North-West London, living my comfortable middle-class life, to go to a comfortable *mikva* like some people go to the local jacuzzi or sauna! In Russia, people have had to build *mikvas* secretly, some of them have built a hidden one in their home, and have had to live constantly with the fear of being discovered by the KGB who would imprison them because of it. Some women in Russia travel hundreds of miles under extraordinarily difficult circumstances, just to get to the *mikva* on time.

It is very important to go to the *mikva* on time, and the woman who puts herself out and goes to the *mikva* even when it is not convenient to go, is commended by the rabbis in Jewish literature. It seems that it might take a great deal of commitment and determination to drag yourself out in the pouring rain or snow, until you think about how much you miss your husband when you cannot even touch him for nearly two weeks. Sometimes there might be the temptation to leave it until the next day if the weather is bad or your car will not start. Occasionally, in spite of the long time which has gone by without so much as a cuddle, you have a dreadful day and you just do not feel in the mood. A friend of mine had one of those awful days at work when she felt like hitting everyone and shouting at everybody in sight. She came home and screamed at her husband. Then she screamed at the children. It was *mikva* night, and the last thing in the world that she felt like doing was making love to her husband – she could have quite cheerfully strangled him! She packed her bag together and drove like a maniac to the *mikva*. She ran her bath, cut her nails viciously one by one. Threw her nails viciously in the bin. She brushed her teeth furiously, combed her hair frantically, and took her make up off, scrubbing her face until it was bright pink. By the time she had finished, she had worked off her aggression and came out of the *mikva* totally relaxed.

When a woman has her period, she may feel unwell, suffer with pre-menstrual tension, period pains, backache and other symptoms. The period of separation from her husband not only gives her an opportunity for physical recuperation, but also gives the couple a chance to relate to each other in a non-physical way. When the woman is *nidda*, or 'separate', her husband cannot touch her. He cannot kiss or cuddle her. The same applies to the woman. The couple cannot use physical contact to avoid conflict, and so have to make friends, talk to each other and negotiate in a non-physical way. This provides a solid foundation for their marriage, which contributes to the comparatively low divorce rate in the religious community. This is because of the continuous cycle of separation and togetherness, when the relationship is constantly being renewed.

When I was pregnant, and we did not have this constantly changing situation of togetherness and separation, my husband complained that I had not noticed him kissing me goodbye in the morning – I was starting to take him for granted after only a few months without going to the *mikva!* It just shows how much people take for granted in contemporary society where kissing has become as ordinary as a handshake and the media are constantly giving us the message that sex is only exciting if it is different or forbidden.

The principle of separation has another beneficial aspect. The woman has to count seven days after her menstrual bleeding has stopped. This brings the time of resuming sexual relations right up to what is for most women the most fertile time of the month. Modern treatment for infertility utilizes this concept, something that the Jewish people have been practising for thousands of years. The separation of husband and wife after childbirth is also beneficial, because the time immediately after giving birth is not usually when a woman feels like having sex, and time can be devoted to bonding with the baby.

Like the dietary laws, which mean that although we should enjoy our food we are limited to certain foods, we are encouraged to enjoy sex, but only in the context of a legal marriage and with certain constraints. If you eat too much, you feel sick. Too much sex becomes boring – sex therapists can testify to many marriages on the rocks because of sexual boredom, and the first stage in therapy is to ban sex. Very often, the actual fact that what had become boring has suddenly become forbidden, makes the couple start to enjoy sex again! To quote my rabbi: 'Masters and Johnson – what did they know about sex that the rabbis didn't know about two thousand years ago?'

In Judaism, the women are certainly not in any way second class or inferior. In fact, the Jewish view is that because they can carry life, women have a much higher spiritual level than men. Women are considered to be 'partners in creating life' and therefore have a close and intuitive link with God. The laws of *mikva* give women an element of power within the marriage relationship and in modern society protect women from becoming sex objects. The orthodox Jews are the only community in this country where sex is on women's terms, and where women can truthfully say that they are not used by their husbands.

So it should be clear that the separation of husband and wife has nothing to do with inferiority of the woman. Dr Marie Stopes, the English doctor who is famous for her work in the 1920s on marital relations said of the Jewish marital laws of *Taharat HaMishpachah:*

> They depict the most advanced lifestyle in the world today, being in total harmony with the functioning of a woman's body. The requirement for abstinence after menstruation and the time for resuming relations correspond precisely to the natural tides of a woman's sexual desire.[1]

The laws of *mikva* have been passed down from mother to daughter in a continuous chain from biblical times. *Mikvas* are being excavated in Israel, and at the top of Massada where the Jewish zealots were besieged by the Romans around two thousand years ago, a *mikva* has been discovered among the ruins. A *mikva* is central to the setting up of a Jewish community, and building a *mikva* is even more of a priority than building a synagogue. The fact that these laws concerning *mikva* have survived until now shows the extent to which the Jewish people have clung to their faith even under adverse circumstances. Even when besieged by the Romans, they built a *mikva* at the top of a high mountain in the desert.

But even more so, the miraculous survival of the Jewish people has mainly been ascribed to their faithful adherence to these laws. As it says in the Torah: 'More than the Jews have kept the Torah, the Torah has kept the Jews.' Because modesty in behaviour is such a high priority, these laws of *Taharat HaMishpachah* have not been publicized, but have been handed down throughout the generations. The laws are kept because of our faith; it is possible to see why they have even been called 'the secret of our survival'.

1 cited in Tehilla Abramov, *The Secret of Jewish Femininity* (New York, Targum Press, 1988), p. 105.

7 *Lavinia Byrne* IBVM

Apart From or A Part Of: The place of celibacy

At the age of seventeen I entered a convent. I was clothed in black from head to toe six weeks after my eighteenth birthday. The part of the convent in which I lived was called the noviceship. It occupied the top floor of a three-storey building, with several levels of what spatial archaeologists call permeability between it and the world outside. We did not speak in the corridors there, indeed after nine o'clock at night we did not speak at all. Our clothes, living space and total environment all separated us from the outer world. They also served to protect our privacy needs. Of course I did not see it like that at the time. I just accepted that that was how it was. When the opportunity came, with the Roman Catholic Church's Second Vatican Council, to get rid of what felt increasingly antiquated, I was keen to give the lead. Out went religious dress and many of the customs and practices which went with wearing it. The convent became more open, family and friends came in to share meals and conversation. Silence became a thing of the past.

Right now I find myself regretting the fact that we have done very little to replace them. These images of separation – the habit, the enclosure and silence – served a two-fold purpose. They enabled the sisters to honour their own privacy needs and they gave us a clear sense of personal identity. They helped individual sisters to enjoy a sense of apartness which many women would envy. They gave members of the group a clear sense of belonging to each other, as part of a shared community, which is equally enviable. We have done little to consider how new members entering the religious life nowadays can internalize the attitudes they attempted to represent. We have done little to attempt to encapsulate this wisdom and offer it to women in general, both within and outside the Church.

And yet why, ultimately, did these particular practices have to be abandoned? I see two principal reasons why this happened. The first has to do with the return to primary sources which the Second Vatican Council recommended. The primary sources for the religious orders were the lives and experience of their first and founding sisters, but equally they were the early sources of Christianity itself, namely the Gospels and the experience of those primitive Christian groups whose stories are depicted in the Acts of the Apostles. The Jerusalem, or Early Church model, began to predominate, and this meant being with people rather than apart from them. A model of Christian living and hence of holiness which relied on images of separation and apartness became highly suspect.

The second reason has to do with a simple fact of communication. The religious habit had lost its symbolic value; it no longer conveyed the meaning it was intended to convey. It had become associated in the popular imagination with something naive, laughable or downright kinky. The stripping traffic warden was joined by the stripping nun in the Kissogram adverts. So too with the convent building. It suddenly appeared rather middle-class, and draughty anyway, with falling numbers of young people entering. Ideologically sound sisters moved to hard-to-let housing in depressed urban centres and sold their properties to hotels and banks. Equally the message conveyed by silence was increasingly one of indifference or even hostility in a world dominated by protest and the call to apostolic action.

Both the external images of apartness and the usefulness of the attitudes they represented were considered questionable. The nuns joined the lemmings and darted over an immense cliff called apostolic activity. Nowadays we are regaining some of our sense of perspective. We are prepared to question some of the cult phrases of the sixties and seventies and the level of involvement they advocated. We stand now at a turning point. We are all too aware that fashions come and go before we have had time to get a grip on the underlying theology which informs them. The experience of the early Christians depicted in Acts was without doubt an experience of release, as they came to abandon practices which they found restrictive, and which had been encapsulated in laws which served to keep the Jews apart from the rest of the nations. The community life and missionary life of the Early Christians meanwhile – their life in the private domain and in the public domain – would be guided by the light of the Spirit. This meant open community and open mission fields. It meant an image of holiness which read the life of discipleship as a call to integration. Community and mission belong together and both mean being with people rather than apart from them. This sounds like an entirely comforting vision of the Church. It finds a place for everyone within the divine purpose, regardless of their background, status or gender.

But if we begin to question the model of integration and belonging, what are the alternatives? The equally monolithic image of the male saint, Demetrios on his charger, is not really for us either. Our dilemma is that it speaks of a level of separation from the world, the flesh and human reality which has already proved far too harmful to the churches in general and for women in particular for us to consider returning to it.

Monolithic notions of sanctity reveal a startling reliance on hierarchical thinking. The saint is the man who has withdrawn from the rough-and-tumble world of everyday living. He is white or, if he is black, a recent convert to the missionary Church and a martyr. He is generally unmarried, even though he may have had a shady past which included associating with women. He is a deeply spiritual man – that is part of his attraction – and he shows true concern for others. He is ordinarily a priest. What is the underlying theology which enables the churches to recognize sanctity in this way? It is based on the assumption that the sacred is better than the secular, that the Church is essentially European and only universal by implication, that celibacy is better than marriage, that belief cannot go hand in hand with doubt, that the clerical state is more sublime than the lay, and hence that women are excluded from belonging at the level at which this belonging is most valued.

Not only is this thinking hierarchical, it is also dualistic. Hidden divisions are taken for granted. They affect our understanding of Christian living – the secular/sacred divide; of Christian mission – the European/rest of the world divide; of Christian morality – the celibacy/marriage divide; of God – the belief/unbelief divide; and of the Church – the clerical/lay divide. The vision proclaimed by Paul in his Letter to the Galatians is totally undermined by moral dualisms he never even envisaged. He had written, 'There are no more distinctions between Jew and Greek, slave and free, male and female, but all of you are one in Christ Jesus' (Gal. 3.28). What an irony! And yet in his own lifetime, there were occasions when Paul too pulled the barriers down again. For Christianity can never deny its Jewish origins. A monotheistic God is a God who insists on being 'over against' and separate from creation and from the gods of other nations. But this basic dualism in Judeo-Christian thought must not be understood as a moral dualism. And our dilemma is that this is precisely what we do with it.

Indeed, hierarchical ways of organizing Church reality have become so normative that we do not ordinarily stop to examine them. Only present-day interest in a spirituality for all the baptized can force us to ask questions about them. For not only are they bad for women – who find it difficult to be canonized unless they are nuns, queens or martyrs – but equally they form another monolith. This does not replicate the monolithic vision of the Early Church but it is characterized by the same overall patterns. Where the Early Church had a vision of community and mission as its sustaining theology, a hierarchical Church has an equally well-organized vision, only this time it is a vision of separation. Both leave unanswered questions however, because both are overly monolithic. They force us to choose between being a part of or apart from the world of our everyday living.

So where are we to go? The nuns and their secular sisters have a common task; we share a common quest both for a way forward and for appropriate role models.

Celibacy is interesting because it is counter-cultural. It enables women who choose not to get married but rather to live in religious community to side-step issues which haunt and dominate present-day society. Male behaviour is so normative that we ordinarily think of celibacy as meaning that men are to leave women alone, rather than seeing it as a positive step women take to make a non sexually-active community together. There are negative images of celibacy of course, and the Christian Churches are as much to blame for propagating these as anyone else.

The most negative is the image of renunciation. According to this understanding, people who make vows of celibacy are somehow standing in judgement over those who do not. If this were the case, most people, whose call is to marriage, would be able to pick up one message and one message only from celibates. Sex is bad. The better part lies in renouncing it. Yet we know this to be untrue. After all, the Church also teaches that most people bring the divine image to completion within the context of marriage. Here man and woman meet and God is imaged most truly.

Another image is of celibacy as protest. The social gospel is best preached by someone who burns with zeal rather than sexual desire and has espoused God alone. This probably works for some people, but I have to say that I have reservations about it. It is not a good model for human relations, and some of the people who are aflame with political zeal and want to put the entire world to rights are in fact hell to live with. The demands of personal intimacy are demands they are just not prepared to meet.

Then there is the argument about availability. The celibate person is more available, not less so. Because she is not saying 'I love you' to one person, she is free to say it to everyone. This sounds compelling and attractive but it can be promiscuous as well. Neither rejection, protest nor availability prepares us for the demands which celibacy is making on us nowadays.

For celibacy is only really intelligible when understood as a demand of love. When nuns make vows of celibacy they are saying that something is true for them in particular but that it does not belong to them. There are many lay people who share and live out of the same insight. What is being said is that God's love makes its home in human beings and that it seeks to be replicated and brought to completion within them. The metaphor this time is not the one from Genesis which tells how God made us in the divine image, male and female, and that completion lies in the union of men and women. This time the underlying image of God is the image of the Trinity, the communion of love within the Godhead. Celibacy becomes a call to profound but non-sexual intimacy, just as the Father, Son and Holy Spirit enjoy profound non-sexual intimacy. In order to be authentic it has to be lived in the wider context of the real world in which religious women make their vows, informed both by the relationship they enjoy with the God who calls them and the real live people God gives them to love. If it is lived in that world, the vow of celibacy witnesses to other women and indeed to men.

We should not have to apologize for a vow of celibacy. What it is saying is in fact very simple. Things do not have to be as they are. There are other, non-sexual, ways of organizing human reality in general and human relationships in particular.

I have suggested that there are two threads running through

Christian practice, the thread of integration and that of separation, of being a part of and apart from. But equally there is the option of differentiation, which is about setting oneself apart from the norm, not simply to criticize and condemn it but to set up an alternative and different model.

I find myself turning to the first chapter of the Book of Genesis for an insight into what I am hinting at here. The priestly authors who compiled this version of the creation story show us a God who differentiates, who divides the night from the day, the light from the dark. This creative God finds divisions good. This God finds the divine imaged within the human, and notably within what is male and what is female within the human. This God permits diversification and diversity at an essential level. This God allows people to be different from each other – slaves from the free, Jews from Greeks and women from men. The formula is absurdly simple: 'different from' does not mean 'better than'. True vision comes only with the insight of a God who allows differentiation.

At its best, in the 'high age' of religious life, the nuns' lives had the authority that comes from total harmony between inner attitudes and outer forms. Their inner understanding of belonging was mirrored in external images of withdrawal. I envy them this. My own world seems much more complicated.

But differentiation has another meaning as well and this gives me hope. In nature, and in particular in the development of the human embryo, it means specialization. Individual cells have to develop differently in order to make any biological organism. They may all start off the same, but the principle of organization is inexorable and they develop specialized functions according to the needs of the whole. A cell's true nature is realized when it becomes skin or bone or nerve ending. Had this differentiation never taken place the result would be something inconceivably horrible, an amorphous mass of cells with no identity at all. Every cell is needed for the whole to exist. Each cell depends on the ability of others to differentiate and so specialize. If this is true at the micro-level of human physical development, its relevance and worth at the level of human social development cannot be ignored. Furthermore, what is true of the phenomenon of celibacy as a metaphor of an appropriate form of apartness and of integration is also true of individual members of a group such as a religious community. My ability to be part of a greater dissenting whole is balanced by my ability to stand apart and hence to differentiate within the group.

The drama for women, of course, is that we have been encouraged to become dependent and hold others in dependent relationships and have rarely sought to differentiate: womens' groups can be as tyrannical as any other when they do not allow diversity and disagreement. This is why convents are such fascinating places. I am not saying that women religious have totally solved the problem. Indeed in many cases they are a long way away from having done so. Nevertheless I would claim that the religious life as a phenomenon has insights which can throw light on the question, because the nuns have been wrestling with it for centuries.

When I was a postulant, or aspirant young novice, I used to work in the laundry. My fellow novices and I operated an ironing machine. It was hot and heavy work. The laundress, a tough and saintly old German sister, would give out the rosary as we worked. On one occasion I remember that she promoted me very briefly for the space of an entire morning. I was allowed to work on my own rather than in the production line. I was given a pile of sacristy wash rather than vests, sheets and shirts. 'Our Blessed Lord lies here,' she told me as she handed me altar cloths and corporals to iron. There was no higher promotion than that.

When I left the laundry and the kitchen where I received my basic formation as a novice, I went off to university. Gradually I was initiated into other roles. Or rather other functions. My role within the community was always the same. I was a sister. My functions could change – and often did. At one moment I was a novice working in the laundry, at another I was a university student, at another a young teacher, at another a friend, at another an enemy. My basic vocation was assured. The ways in which I lived out this my own appropriate identity within this vocation were diverse.

What I am saying is this. At its best the religious life for women has shown a sure and thorough knowledge of the difference between function models and role models. Function models are important because they enable us to separate tasks and approach them in an organized way. Laundry is important, study is important, teaching is important. In order to teach potential students the value of laundry work you make them do it for a while. Once they have learnt its value, you can train them to develop their own skills. Then they will value the work of people who work at simple domestic tasks. They will never despise them. Because they have learnt to be a part of these tasks it is safe to ask them to differentiate, to take up the specialization which is appropriate to their gifts and skills and interests. Time spent in an embryonic space is not wasted.

But then comes the time of differentiation, the time when the busy teacher takes her clothes down to the laundry on a Saturday morning and flings them in the laundry basket in the confidence that they will be returned neatly pressed later in the week. A guilty middle-class version of feminism would want all the sisters to launder, all the sisters to teach. At its most saintly the religious life offered a much more functional view. There were tasks for everyone which took account of intelligence, educational opportunities and personal gifts. Nowadays we live in less saintly times and I long for someone to help me with my ironing. Indeed I cheat. I wear long-sleeved pullovers and hope no one will notice that only the cuffs and collars of my shirts have been pressed.

There are other examples, of course. My point is that in a single-sex community tasks have to be shared. There are administrators, nurses, accountants, visionaries, teachers, bureaucrats, carers, impressarios, entrepreneurs, cleaners and so on. Each of the sisters who offers an appropriate form of service to the group enables the balance to be held at rest. Each of these is asked to be part of the community and yet to develop her own specialization. The value of a religious noviciate which asks novices to try out a variety of these functions in turn is that it exposes novices to the value of each. Never again will they imagine that to be an administrator is to be superior to being a cleaner. Never again will they be sentimental and imagine that being a cleaner is superior to being an administrator. Both functions make different demands. Both are needed within the body.

Is this a return to dualisms? Does it conceal a kind of romantic fascism, where everyone has a proper state and none should aspire to alter or change this state? My answer is No. The hierarchical way of moral dualisms is based uniquely in separation, whereas the underlying theology of a religious community is the life of the Trinity itself. Here relationships are ordered, certainly; each person of the Trinity has a differentiated function, but all are equal. The Life-giver, Pain-bearer and Comforter are three persons and they are God. They are apart from each other and part of each other. Theirs is a totally relational model of being and doing in which domination and jealousy and separation are unknown. The life of the Godhead is a life of mutual support and self-gift. It is a hidden life, a life of privacy; but equally it is a life of total intimacy, a life lived in love.

I would now like to turn to the symbol of the Virgin Mary in the light of this discussion. As a role model, she is a highly contentious one. She has been hopelessly sentimentalized and hopelessly magicalized by tradition, with the result that Christian feminism has come to be uncomfortable with her. (Mary Magdalen is found to be an altogether more sympathetic role model; she has a nice plain earthiness which seems to make more sense of our actual lived experience.) And yet in our quest for holiness, the title 'virgin mother' holds the key.

Mary is virgin and mother. If we persist in interpreting virginity and motherhood only in a physical sense this leaves us with a problem, and she once again becomes a burden by being an impossible act to follow. But if the reality is allowed to stand but is also understood as a metaphor for the experience of all women, then I believe Mary can speak to our condition.

For beyond biological virginity and motherhood lie the metaphor of virginity, which is about separation, and the metaphor of motherhood, which is about integration. A woman who holds both of these in balance demonstrates the sanctifying power of differentiation. She is both apart from and part of the human condition. The virgin is the reserved figure who does not define herself in terms of her relationships with men. She is autonomous. The mother, meanwhile, is essentially in relationship. The virgin is barren through choice or misfortune. Her energy is inner-directed. The mother is fecund. She is creative of life and ongoing nurture. Mary the mother of Jesus is represented in Christian art in terms of both these images. Depictions of the Annunciation show her alone. The angel Gabriel is sent by God to a virgin in a town in Galilee called Nazareth. To gain access to her he has to penetrate many layers of permeability. Depictions of the nativity meanwhile show her with her son, with Joseph, the angels, the ox and the ass, the shepherds and the magi: with all the characters who make up the Christmas story. The star is there as well, a reminder of the cosmic importance of God's intervention in the life of the virgin mother. Mary is holy because God gives her both these roles, enables her to hold them both in balance and empowers her desires and choices from this point of balance.

Where does all this leave us present-day women? Firstly, I believe, it offers us an interesting way of interpreting images of seclusion and withdrawal. These do not necessarily represent a kind of tyranny imposed by men on women. Where the veil, the cloister and silence are freely chosen, they can guarantee a degree of apartness which is highly desirable. This is true of their contemporary equivalents as well. Women are entitled to space both in the domestic context and in the public domain. Where some women are free to make vows of chastity, we are reminded that all women should be free to refuse men access to them. The expression 'conjugal rights' gains a new and more reciprocal kind of meaning. But secondly it highlights the fact that women are entitled to the freedom to engage with and be part of all the creative, nurturing processes with which we organize human reality. The mistake would be for the one to cancel out the other. We are invited to be open to the choices each of them represents. This is not to set up a system which once again asks women to do something painful and impossible, to juggle with all the expectations that come when we are working as wives and mothers and outside the home as well. Rather it suggests that women should be allowed to differentiate. This differentiation puts us in a place of desire and of choice. It enables us to experience desires we do not ordinarily give ourselves credit for, and to exercise choices society is reluctant to admit. If celibacy and the life of professed religious women are about anything at all, they are about this hidden strand both within the Christian tradition in particular and in women's lives in general.